INTRODUCTORY LECTURES ON LACAN

THE CENTRE FOR FREUDIAN ANALYSIS AND RESEARCH LIBRARY

Series Editors:
Anouchka Grose, Darian Leader, Alan Rowan

CFAR was founded in 1985 with the aim of developing Freudian and Lacanian psychoanalysis in the UK. Lacan's rereading and rethinking of Freud had been neglected in the Anglophone world, despite its important implications for the theory and practice of psychoanalysis. Today, this situation is changing, with a lively culture of training groups, seminars, conferences, and publications.

CFAR offers both introductory and advanced courses in psychoanalysis, as well as a clinical training programme in Lacanian psychoanalysis. It can provide access to Lacanian psychoanalysts working in the UK, and has links with Lacanian groups across the world. The CFAR Library aims to make classic Lacanian texts available in English for the first time, as well as publishing original research in the Lacanian field.

OTHER TITLES IN THE SERIES

- *Lacan and Lévi-Strauss or The Return to Freud (1951–1957)*
  by Markos Zafiropoulos
- *The Trainings of the Psychoanalyst*
  by Annie Tardits
- *Sexual Ambiguities*
  by Geneviève Morel
- *Freud and the Desire of the Psychoanalyst*
  by Serge Cottet
- *Lacan: The Unconscious Reinvented*
  by Colette Soler

www.cfar.org.uk

INTRODUCTORY LECTURES ON LACAN

Edited by
Astrid Gessert

Routledge
Taylor & Francis Group
LONDON AND NEW YORK

First published 2014 by Karnac Books Ltd.

Published 2018 by Routledge
2 Park Square, Milton Park, Abingdon, Oxon OX14 4RN
711 Third Avenue, New York, NY 10017, USA

Routledge is an imprint of the Taylor & Francis Group, an informa business

Copyright © 2014 to Astrid Gessert for the edited collection, and to the individual authors for their contributions.

The rights of the contributors to be identified as the authors of this work have been asserted in accordance with §§ 77 and 78 of the Copyright Design and Patents Act 1988.

All rights reserved. No part of this book may be reprinted or reproduced or utilised in any form or by any electronic, mechanical, or other means, now known or hereafter invented, including photocopying and recording, or in any information storage or retrieval system, without permission in writing from the publishers.

Notice:
Product or corporate names may be trademarks or registered trademarks, and are used only for identification and explanation without intent to infringe.

British Library Cataloguing in Publication Data

A C.I.P. for this book is available from the British Library

ISBN-13: 9781782201083 (pbk)

Typeset by V Publishing Solutions Pvt Ltd., Chennai, India

To the students of CFAR and "mon grand assistant"

CONTENTS

ABOUT THE EDITOR AND CONTRIBUTORS　　　　　ix

INTRODUCTION　　　　　xi

CHAPTER ONE
The unconscious from Freud to Lacan　　　　　1
Anouchka Grose

CHAPTER TWO
The place of the mirror phase in Lacan's work　　　　　23
Gerry Sullivan

CHAPTER THREE
The object from Freud to Lacan　　　　　39
Noga Wine

CHAPTER FOUR
Hysteria and obsession　　　　　55
Astrid Gessert

CHAPTER FIVE
An introductory journey in transference   69
Vincent Dachy

CHAPTER SIX
Interpretation   83
Darian Leader

INDEX   95

ABOUT THE EDITOR AND CONTRIBUTORS

Vincent Dachy practises and teaches Lacanian psychoanalysis in London. He is a member of the Centre for Freudian Analysis and Research (CFAR) and of The London Society of the New Lacanian School. Aside from psychoanalysis he writes texts in association with photographs, and reciprocally, between prose and poetry.

Astrid Gessert is a practising psychoanalyst and a member of CFAR and of The College of Psychoanalysts-UK. She is a regular contributor to the CFAR public lecture and training programme and lectures and facilitates seminars at other psychoanalytic organisations.

Anouchka Grose is a writer and psychoanalyst practising in London. Her books include, *No More Silly Love Songs: A Realist's Guide to Romance* (Portobello, 2010) and *Are You Considering Therapy?* (Karnac, 2011).

Darian Leader is a psychoanalyst working in London and a founder member of CFAR. He is President of The College of Psychoanalysts-UK and Visiting Professor at the School of Human and Life Sciences, Roehampton University. He is the author of several books including: *Introducing Lacan*; *Why Do Women Write More Letters than They Post?*;

Freud's Footnotes; *Stealing the Mona Lisa: What Art Stops Us From Seeing*; *Why Do People Get Ill?* (with David Corfield); *The New Black: Mourning, Melancholia and Depression*, and *What is Madness?* His most recent book, *Strictly Bipolar*, is published by Hamish Hamilton, 2013.

Gerry Sullivan is a psychoanalyst working in private practice and a member of CFAR. He lectures widely on psychoanalysis and contributes to CFAR's seminar programme.

Noga Wine is a psychoanalyst practising in Rio de Janeiro, Brazil. She is a member of CFAR and of The London Society of the New Lacanian School. She has a Ph.D. in psychoanalysis from the Federal University of Rio de Janeiro, Instituto de Psicologia.

INTRODUCTION

This book contains a selection of introductory lectures about some of the fundamental concepts of psychoanalysis from a Lacanian perspective. The topics range from some of Freud's basic metapsychological concepts to questions of neurosis and clinical structure, and psychoanalytic technique. The lectures were presented by members of the Centre for Freudian Analysis and Research (CFAR) and attracted a mixed audience of people from all walks of life, including practising psychoanalysts and psychotherapists of various orientations, people engaged in art, literature, media, social and cultural studies, students and teachers from academia and the clinical field, and others interested in questions of psychoanalysis and Lacanian theory and practice. The idea of publishing a selection of writings from the lecture programme arose in response to the lively interest shown by the audience and frequent requests for the papers presented.

Each lecture, on a topic of psychoanalysis, is self-contained. Our aim has been to show how Freud's understanding of some of the key concepts of psychoanalysis have been revised and developed by Lacan. The framework chosen for these explorations, in the form of individual lectures on each topic, does not allow for a full account of the historical development or indeed for a comprehensive exploration of the concept in question. It was left to the individual speakers to present what aspects they thought would be of particular interest and value. In the articles collected we tried to retain the liveliness of the spoken discourse and the peculiarity of each speaker. Some of the contributors are not native English speakers which is reflected in their language and has been corrected only to the point of ensuring a smoother reading and avoiding misunderstandings due to language problems. We were also interested in exposing complexities, questions, uncertainties, and gaps rather than in presenting a, perhaps more gratifying but ultimately problematic, appearance of simplicity, completeness, and finality. As the CFAR Introductory Lecture Programme has been running for over two decades the present selection presents the understanding individual speakers have developed of their topics over a period of time. It cannot be assumed that this process will stop here and that the texts will be the "final word".

The introductory lecture programme is presented at CFAR every academic year on a fortnightly schedule, with different speakers addressing the selected topics each time round. The selection of topics varies and includes, in addition to the topics covered in this book, the following themes: the Oedipus complex, identification, the image and the ego, the drive, unconscious phantasy, gender, psychosis, the symbolic, the imaginary and the real, the subject and the Other, and the variable length session. There are always lively discussions with the audience asking questions and providing comments, often offering interesting perspectives from their own fields of expertise.

The intention of the book is not to provide another "Introduction to Lacan" or to be in competition with the many excellent introductory texts that are available on this subject. It is intended for the large group of interested readers who, no matter if inspired by enthusiasm or scepticism, are curious about the peculiarities of psychoanalysis and Lacan's engagement with it. Those readers who are familiar with psychoanalytic literature and the teaching of Lacan may find little that is new to them, but they will encounter some interesting perspectives and points of presentation that may direct them along pathways less explored, and encourage them in pursuing their own subjective ways of engaging further with psychoanalysis and the work of Jacques Lacan.

I would like to express very special thanks to the speakers who contributed their lectures for this publication and gave so generously of their time; equal thanks goes to the audience whose lively interest and participation in discussions has contributed significantly to the development of psychoanalytic thinking within CFAR. Without Darian Leader's tireless encouragement during periods when the process of collecting the material was flagging, and his very generous help with editorial questions and with improving the readability of some of the articles whose authors are not native English speakers, the book would never have materialised. A great "Thank you" goes to him. I am also thanking Oliver Rathbone from Karnac for his ongoing encouragement and support of the book and its publication.

Astrid Gessert

CHAPTER ONE

The unconscious from Freud to Lacan

Anouchka Grose

It's not just in the pub that you meet people who say they don't believe in the unconscious; you also get them on the couch. There is a popular idea that Freud is so outdated and disproven that psychoanalysis surely can't be about all that. If someone knows they've made a Freudian slip, the recognition that they've done so can almost appear to annul it. It becomes a joke, "Ha ha, I just said one thing and meant my mother". Knowledge of psychoanalysis is put at the service of defence.

Familiarity with the notion of the unconscious, and all the debate that has sprung up around it—plus the current mania for encouraging people to believe they can control everything in their own lives—means that people are possibly better defended against the concept than they were a hundred years ago. They can see it coming a mile off and can draw on a battalion of reasons not to take it seriously. But still they have symptoms that bring them to therapy. Perhaps the hope is that there will be a number of "nice" ego-syntonic reasons why they're suffering— because so and so was horrible to them and it's not fair, and therapy will help them to get over it. There are plenty of therapies that will aim to do exactly that. But going to psychoanalysis would imply that the unconscious is going to be taken seriously, which is going to mean there's a high chance you might be led to think about things you'd rather not think about; as in, really rather not think about. Which is obviously a strange experience to put yourself through voluntarily.

I will try to describe the mechanics of the unconscious as outlined by Freud. Things often seem to go wrong when the unconscious is depicted as something a bit blurry. Of course the contents of your own unconscious might seem a bit blurry (thanks to repression) but Freud's concept isn't. It's easier to defend oneself against it when it all looks a bit messy and weird. So for clinicians it's important to try to be precise about the machinations of the unconscious, and not be terrorised by people's suspicions around it. But first maybe it's useful to say a bit about the pre-history of Freud's ideas.

The "discovery" of the unconscious

There's a good deal of debate about how much credit Freud deserves. Did he "discover" the unconscious? Did he steal the idea from his colleagues? How did the theory come about? Freud himself said, in a short, posthumously published essay, "The concept of the unconscious has long been knocking at the gates of psychology and asking to be let in." (1940b, p. 286) According to Freud, the idea had been lurking around in philosophy and literature for centuries, but science hadn't known what to do with it. Freud found a way to talk about it and to theorise it. So there's no claim from Freud that it's a big innovation of his, just that he found a different way to think and speak about it.

Before Freud you have a long history of people trying to understand mysterious symptoms, particularly in women. Why were these things happening that had no obvious organic cause? The way of thinking about it—and treating it—was most often that it had something to do with sex. Women were prescribed "massages" (masturbation by a doctor) in the hope that an orgasm would make them better. This treatment was so common—and impractical—that the Victorians invented clockwork vibrators to get the job done more efficiently. There was no mention of an unconscious in any of this, but a big question about why these mysterious things happened. Was it demons, gases in the womb, no sex or no babies? Did it only happen to women? And so on.

Outside medicine you had the perfectly commonplace idea that people might do or say things without knowing why. They might also think about things they didn't want to think about, or keep getting into situations that made them suffer, or they might do self-destructive things. But how to understand all that? There was the classic question of fate *vs.* personal responsibility. Was there an external force, like God, that threw things in your way and made you miserable in order to teach you something? Were you master of your own destiny? Could you control your actions and feelings? There were endless debates about passion *vs.* reason. Is it best to contain your feelings and try to behave rationally, or does that make you a hollow or desiccated person? Is it better to live according to your emotions, even if you don't know why you have those emotions? Countless philosophical essays, novels, poems, and paintings try to say something about whether people are rational, controlled beings or uncontrollable balls of sentiment. So, there are these big questions about who's in charge, and lots of interest in the question, but none of it particularly scientific.

Immediately preceding Freud there were four very important figures in the medical world looking into questions about the mechanics of the mind. Charcot was a famous neurologist at Salpêtrière Hospital who developed the idea that some of the physical symptoms he was seeing in the hospital were caused by what he called "traumatic hysteria". People would arrive suffering from a variety of seizures, pains, and contractures and his innovation was to link their symptoms to traumatic events in their past—maybe accidents or crashes. Perhaps they even sustained real injuries as a result of these accidents, but Charcot concluded that it was the unsettling idea of the accident that was the cause of their ongoing illness. He also thought that hysteria had a hereditary component. Freud studied with Charcot in the mid 1880s and was obviously impressed and influenced by him.

Thanks to Charcot, the diagnosis of hysteria became very fashionable—anything a bit strange or hard to explain would fall into that category. So here was a super-famous doctor, giving quite spectacular demonstrations. He would induce a hysterical state using hypnosis. There's a well-known painting by Andre Brouillet showing a woman collapsing in front of Charcot and a room full of very interested doctors. The medical establishment had previously been rather suspicious of hypnosis, thanks to associations with Mesmer, who was seen as pretty suspect. Charcot's experiments brought it into the medical mainstream. He attempted to use it both as a cure and as a device to demonstrate the difference between normal and hysterical states. People could be induced to act "hysterically" under hypnosis.

So Charcot was launching himself into a hot debate in an exciting way and sort of spewing ideas out and getting everyone interested. Many of his students took up his ideas, like Freud, Pierre Janet, and Hyppolite Bernheim (who were all interested in hypnosis), as well as Tourette, and a number of others who went on to become important in the medical world. But it wasn't just the medical establishment who was impressed; there was also huge interest from outside.

Hysteria, in the sense in which Charcot and his contemporaries understood it, is now seen by many people in the medical profession as having been a very problematic diagnosis. People who would now be diagnosed with concussion or epilepsy were having their symptoms put down to hysteria. This is one of the things people, like Richard Webster, conjure all sorts of things out of when they want to attack Freud. The basic logic of this attack is as follows: Charcot was wrong, therefore Freud—who was influenced by him—is wrong. It's hardly the most watertight logic.

Pierre Janet was a student of Charcot's in the late eighteen hundreds. He coined the term "subconscient" in order to talk about the "splitting of the mind". This was, according to Janet, a phenomenon you might see in hysteria, and also in hypnosis. He also introduced the term "dissociation" to describe how a person dissociates themselves from a traumatic experience. He used both of those ideas to try to say something about amnesia. How do lost memories come about? And again, what's the place of amnesia and dissociation in hysteria? Like Charcot, he used hypnosis both as an investigative tool and also as a form of treatment. You often hear that Janet deserves much more credit than he gets for the discovery and theorisation of the unconscious. People sometimes like to claim that he's the real genius and Freud just nicked his ideas. As the story goes, Janet was less good at roping in a gang of doctors and writers to disseminate his ideas—because Freud made more of a song and dance about it, he managed to claim the credit.

Janet also developed a theory of transference to account for the fact that people became attached to a certain hypnotist and, as a result, would be unhypnotisable by someone else. Janet was younger than Freud, but initially more eminent. Freud was clearly interested in Janet's research, in a competitive way. Anna Freud doesn't mention him at all in her introduction to Freud's essay on the unconscious—but she does mention Charcot, Bernheim, and Breuer.

Hippolyte Bernheim was a French neurologist, practising from the late 1860s. Working in Nancy, he was engaged in experimenting with hypnosis. Bernheim was interested in suggestion, and the fact that it's so amplified under hypnosis. He performed experiments like telling someone, while they are in a hypnotic trance, that they would perform a certain action half an hour later. When they came out of the trance they would go about their business, but when the time came they would go and do exactly as they had been told. If someone asked them why they were doing it they'd make something up. They had no conscious awareness of the fact that they were obeying an order. His experiments show very clearly that people can be pushed to act by ideas that aren't available to consciousness.

The last big influence was Joseph Breuer, and his work with hysterical patients. Hypnosis was being used by Breuer both as a "cure"—"you will no longer have your symptom"—but also as a way to access lost memories. Taking Charcot's idea that hysteria is a result of trauma, patients were invited to bring the traumatic scene back to consciousness in order to "abreact" it—to drain it of its excessive emotional content. In early hypnoanalysis, you have this idea of catharsis as cure. Then of course there was Breuer's rather disastrous treatment of Anna O, after which he lost his stomach for these new ideas and forms of treatment.

The Freudian unconscious

So, Freud took all of these ideas that were very much in the air at the turn of the century and eventually came up with his own, much more developed, theory of the unconscious. In his early case studies of hysterics you see all the usual 1890s stuff—splitting of consciousness, the search for trauma, shock, and nasty surprises. The idea of trauma around sex is included in the set of possibilities, but certainly not privileged. Freud was still using hypnosis, both to give support to suggestion and as a means of opening up access to memories. But by the late 1890s Freud stopped using hypnosis when free association came to seem a better way to tease out unconscious material. In 1898 he published his paper on the sexual aetiology of the neuroses (He had already written "Project for a scientific psychology" in 1895, which contains so many of the ideas he went on to develop later).

By the late 1890s Freud had both the technique of psychoanalysis and also a pretty good early sketch of the theory. He published *The Interpretation of Dreams* in 1900, and in Chapter VII he gave a schematic account of the relations between the conscious, preconscious, and unconscious systems. He developed the idea that unconscious ideas have to attach themselves to preconscious ideas in order to avoid repression, and that this is what leads to the sorts of distortions and peculiarities you see in dreams. In a sense, the whole book is about the unconscious and its relation to consciousness, although the idea itself doesn't get an explicit mention until a couple of hundred pages in. And it's actually not till towards the end that he really tries to say something about the various agencies of the mind and the dynamics at work between them. But you see over the next few years that he does all this amazing work that's been made possible by this new way of thinking about the unconscious. From there he writes *The Psychopathology of Everyday Life* (1901b), *Jokes and Their Relation to the Unconscious* (1905c), and the case histories (1895d), and becomes very famous. He and Carl Jung go to America to talk about the unconscious, and the president is very interested in their work, and so on. Freud, by this time, has quite a collection of followers and fellow researchers. But maybe because the unconscious is such a strange and difficult idea, the more it spread, the more people were liable to misunderstand it. Within psychoanalysis there was a terrible rift with Carl Jung, who'd been so important at the beginning in terms of giving support to Freud's ideas. This was triggered by the fact that Jung developed a notion of the unconscious which showed that he really hadn't taken what Freud had been saying for the last decade all that seriously.

In 1912 Jung published *On the Psychology of the Unconscious*, where it's very plain to see the differences concerning the nature of the libido. You had Freud's theory of the drives and repression, leading to the organisation of the psychic functions into conscious and unconscious processes. Then you had Jung's idea of the libido as a kind of psychic energy that can be channelled towards making you a healthy, creative individual. The idea of the unconscious as a wholesome, natural force that you can tap into in order to live in greater harmony with the world must have been a notion that was appalling to Freud, who really wanted to try to say something precise about the unconscious and didn't want people with woolly spiritual ideas to get in the way.

The split with Jung was acrimonious, and both Freud and Jung seemed to suffer a great deal as a result of it. Jung had a breakdown, Freud collapsed in public in Jung's presence, and made snotty references to him in his work (for instance, in the 1914 paper "On narcissism" (1914c) where Freud points out how stupid and wrong Jung is).

Jung's "wrongness" leaves a huge legacy. His ideas became very popular. Without Jung there would certainly be no *Star Wars* and possibly no *Avatar*. His romantic idea of the unconscious took over where Rousseau left off, and plenty of people seemed to like it.

In 1915 Freud wrote his metapsychological essay on "The unconscious" (1915e). In it, the notion of the unconscious is stripped of its imaginary dimensions (to use a Lacanianism). He tries to talk about it purely in terms of dynamics, topography, and economics. In other words, there are no exciting vignettes or examples, no funny dreams, no little stories about daily life, just a description of the workings of the three systems—the unconscious, the preconscious, and the conscious. Everything is stripped back to bare bones. He's not only correcting potential misunderstandings, but also arguing a case for the unconscious. Of course, there's the problem of trying to speak scientifically about something that can't be measured or proven. Still, Freud claims it's nonetheless necessary—there's enough evidence of this thing, he says, in slips and dreams, and also in symptoms. Symptoms are a place where people find themselves doing things that they can't possibly understand or find any reason for. So Freud states that it really is observably the case that we are capable of psychical activity of which we know nothing, and no amount of angry philosophers can prove otherwise.

Freud describes three systems: unconscious, preconscious, and conscious, with the possibility of transfer of material between them. The conscious deals with the things we know we know. The preconscious handles the things we might know or think about at some point, we just don't happen to be thinking about them at the moment (although if we did want to think about them there'd be no obstacle to their entering into consciousness). Finally there's the unconscious—which houses ideas that are unacceptable to the ego, that need to be kept out of consciousness.

For an idea to make its way from the unconscious into consciousness it would need to pass through the preconscious system. If the idea was deemed not OK for whatever reason, this system would spot it as a no go and keep it back. In other words, the material would be repressed. So the preconscious can hold ideas back, without the conscious mind being made aware of it. This explains what Freud means when he talks about the unconscious part of the ego. The ego isn't analogous with consciousness—there are parts of the ego that can cause unwanted ideas to vanish without us ever being consciously aware of what's going on.

How are we supposed to think about these agencies? Is it simply a poetic idea? Or do they inhabit different areas of the brain? These questions remained unanswerable for Freud, although he didn't deny that answers might become available later. At the time he just said that you can see these functions at work in people, and if science wants to come along later and have something to say about why, then it can. In the meantime the thing is to understand as much as possible about the dynamics of the mind; and the method of psychoanalysis (i.e., free association) provides a perfectly workable tool for doing this. And, anyhow, some kind of evidence for the unconscious had already been provided by hypnotic experiments showing that people could perfectly well be made to perform certain actions without knowing why.

What characterises an unconscious idea? To answer this you would need to untangle the distinction between an instinctual impulse and an unconscious idea. There is a common misconception (perhaps reinforced by Jung) that the unconscious is a place where all the drives are packed off in a swirling state, waiting to burst into action. But Freud says you can't have a notion of the drive in a freeform state, it has to attach itself to an idea, otherwise we really wouldn't know anything about it. So, whether in the unconscious or in the conscious mind, a drive can only be represented by an idea. Therefore, if you talk about unconscious instinctual impulses you are already necessarily talking about unconscious ideas.

There's an interesting section in the essay where Freud says that if you talk about a "repressed instinctual impulse" then "the looseness of phraseology is a harmless one" (ibid., p. 177). But maybe it isn't so harmless, because it's a subject around which there seems to be a lot of room for misunderstanding—which he's supposedly trying to clear up. The idea that the drives are just waiting there, like racehorses in the stalls, might not be exactly how he wants us to see it. He's trying to tell us that the drive has to be linked with an idea in order to be recognised at all. So that's very different from a ball of free-floating primal energy, of the sort you might imagine if you read Jung.

From there, Freud goes on to talk about unconscious emotions—people being in love and not wanting to admit it, or hating, or being envious. How does that sort of thing work? You have drives which are always pushing for satisfaction. So there's a push towards an object that promises to satisfy the drive. Once you have the drive plus the object it's the same as saying you have an idea. According to these systems that allow or disallow ideas there's no such thing as an unacceptable drive, the problem is when the drive attaches itself to the wrong object. If you feel a sexual tug towards a family member, say, you might rather not know about it. It's an anathema to your ego. So your psyche has to go to work to make the idea as harmless as possible. If the thought is pushing to get from the unconscious to the preconscious, and it's being repressed or held back, then there are several possible options. One is that the drive can attach itself to a new object—one which shares enough features with the old object to make for a satisfactory substitute. So you could fall in love with your boss or teacher or some guy who shares a feature with your dad. In these cases the feeling itself isn't repressed, just the idea associated with it.

Alternatively, the affect—the feeling—might take on a different quality of a similar intensity. Typically this would be anxiety. So instead of feeling love or excitement you just feel anxious. Or then again another strategy would be to try to squash the feeling out of existence by denying it. So the unconscious has a number of options for dealing with unwanted affects and ideas. It can displace affect onto a substitute, or it can alter the nature of the affect. But there's always the possibility that the preconscious will see it coming and will try to block it completely. Very often, it simply won't go away. Most often what you will see is a combination of all these strategies. Perhaps there's an attempt to find a new object, but the new object can't replace the old object altogether. As well as covering it, it also invokes it or reminds us of it. So the new object provokes anxiety because it still isn't safe for us to feel the original affect. Then the person may attempt to explain and avoid the anxiety. So it's generally not just one solution or strategy, but a combination.

The unconscious and symptom formation

In the formation of symptoms, consciousness looks for a new object to which to attach the affect. You can maybe see an analogy with hypnosis and the subject's attempts to explain odd actions. It's the same mechanism. A person is hypnotised in an empty room, but they are told to imagine that it's full of furniture. When they come to they will walk around the furniture. They are also told that they won't remember being hypnotised. After they are woken up from their hypnotic trance there's a knock at the door. They go to answer the door, avoiding the imaginary furniture. When asked why they took such a strange route to the door, they make up a story to explain why they didn't walk in a straight line. Their conscious mind rationalises the peculiar action.

So, in a case where affect has been transformed into anxiety, you might see precisely the same kind of trick. Consciousness needs to find a reason why you feel anxious and will cast around for anything that will do. To give a clinical example, you have a woman who has recently changed her life in a certain way—she's got herself out of a relationship in which she seemed to be keeping something going in order to avoid something else. But having got out of the initial set-up there's the risk of suddenly being confronted by this something else. She feels a terrible sense of free-floating anxiety and really doesn't know what to do with herself. Then she hears a bang in the night and becomes absolutely terrified. She has to get her father to come and rescue her. So now she finds herself living in her parents' house, too terrified to go home. The inexplicable flood of anxiety is converted into a fear of intruders, which seems to make it much easier to live with. Plus it gets her back into her parents' house. It's a brilliant solution that seems to let the unconscious have its way at the same time as keeping consciousness happy—a truly ingenious compromise formation.

In section IV of his essay on the unconscious Freud talks about exactly this sort of thing—how a symptom can be formed out of a compromise or stalemate between the three systems of the mind. He takes the workings of phobia apart. In this account there are no horses or penises or mummies on the loo, or any of the interesting phenomena of daily life that are so seductive in the case of Little Hans. He is basically telling the story of Little Hans, but without Little Hans in it.

Freud tells us that a phobia begins with an unacceptable, libidinally invested idea. This idea isn't allowed to pass into consciousness, so the cathexis needs to attach itself to something new. This new idea then becomes a cause of anxiety due to its intimate connection with the repressed idea, and the resulting anxiety has to be prevented or subdued—it needs to be kept out of consciousness. Things further and further removed from the substituted idea trigger mini-warnings, as if to keep the person away from the central, unsettling notion. The ego acts as though the threat comes from outside rather than inside—and that's why the mechanisms prove quite useless. They don't save you from the thing you are trying to avoid, but instead serve as a constant reminder of it.

To give a brief example, which is very similar to the other case I mentioned: we have a woman with a fear of intruders. There was a central fear that a man would break into her house and attack her in her sleep. But there certainly didn't need to be any real sign that this might be happening to set the anxiety off—no banging at the door, no rattling at the window. When it got dark, everything could be a trigger for the fear. A curtain might be hiding something behind it. A light-bulb might suggest a scene from a horror movie. A kitchen would be a place full of dangerous weapons. A bathroom was like the bathroom in the film *Psycho*. At the time it would all seem very real, but then she would wake up the next day and find it completely amazing that she'd been so afraid of her own curtains or of her bedside lamp.

It gradually transpired in analysis that she'd felt like she didn't get enough of her father's attention, and that she desperately craved it. She competed with her mother, believing that the father wasn't satisfied by the mother—although they had never been secretive about their sex life. There were lots of signs that the father was very interested in women and images of women, and in sex in general. So we're looking at a fairly classical Oedipal scenario where the daughter might have all sorts of difficult thoughts and feelings around her father, about which she feels very guilty and ashamed.

When this woman reached her early twenties all of her Oedipal stuff crystallised into a fear of a man coming into her bedroom at night and attacking her. So the sexual excitement became anxiety, and the role of the father was played by the stranger. She tried very hard not to think about any of this—so if the manifest fear was of her curtains when she was alone at night, then she just had to go and stay at a friend's house and she wouldn't have to deal with the curtains any more. It's much easier, or so it appears, to run away from your flat than to run away from your unfortunate sexual phantasy.

But, as Freud puts it, this new fear "proves obdurate and exaggerated" (ibid., p. 183) because it doesn't budge in the face of rationalisation. That's how you can see that it is derived from the unconscious—which makes a bit of a mockery of those treatments, like CBT, that treat symptoms as though they can be rationalised out of existence. Perhaps in a case like this the woman would be cajoled into accepting that there's nothing scary about her light-bulb, and perhaps also that break-ins are extremely rare. But talking to her about crime statistics isn't going to help her with her repressed wishes. This is the obvious danger of quick, rationalising "cures", and explains the frequency of relapse.

Also, in a case like this, you can see the paradoxical nature of the symptom. You want to run away from an idea at the same time as you want to enjoy it. When the affect becomes spread all over everything then you get to feel it all the time, to be reminded of it and to really make it central to your life. So at the same time as you don't "know" anything about your repressed wish, it comes to rule over large chunks of your existence. If the drives are always pushing for discharge, then unconscious ideas linked to the drives will always be fighting for some kind of recognition, through symptoms or in slips or dreams.

If that's how it works in phobia then it's something very similar, Freud says, in conversion hysteria, where you might see how a physical symptom—an ache or a muscle problem—expresses the aim of an impulse at the same time as punishing the person for their unacceptable wish. And then again in a situation where the symptom takes the form of an unhappy relationship. To give one more example, we have a woman who found herself in a very destructive, violent relationship. There's a repressed incestuous wish (although, of course, this only transpires much later, in analysis). She manages to find someone with various father-like features. The partner's initials were the same as her father's and he looked like her father did in wedding photos from before she was born. She tries to insist that her partner proves he loves her in a unique way and that she's different to all other women. He's a very volatile person and blows up at her from time to time—they have physical fights—but he's also madly jealous, which gives her the sense that she must be extremely valuable to him. So she manages to get something of this all-consuming, complete love at the same time as being punished for it. She also feels very much like a victim, and like he is the baddie—so the problem comes from outside not from inside. But it doesn't really work as a long-term solution because she's desperately unhappy, afraid that the violence will escalate and that she'll be seriously hurt.

So repression causes the impulse to be distorted into a form more acceptable to the ego—she's a victim not a disgusting, bad person—but this then puts her in proper danger and, after almost a decade, she realises that she can't live like that. It's the job of the ego to protect us from real dangers too.

You can see in this case that there's a certain level of mental gymnastics required in order to allow the impulse a degree of satisfaction at the same time as placating the ego. When Freud talks about the special characteristics of the unconscious he says there's no negation, no doubt, no varying degrees of certainty, and also no time. All these "realistic" tendencies are introduced by the system preconscious. In the unconscious there is simply an impulse and an idea, and then this has to be knocked into some sort of civilised shape by the other psychic agencies.

In section VI of the essay, Freud talks about communication between the systems. Apparently there's a lot. The unconscious constantly influences the preconscious, which impacts on consciousness. Because the unconscious has the capacity to transform and displace ideas and affects, unconscious derivatives will constantly be making their way into the preconscious and conscious systems. The unconscious is very active, every bit as much so as the other systems.

Freud also refers, near the end of the essay, to unconscious impulses achieving "a high degree of organisation" (ibid., p. 193). This is an idea that will become especially important for Lacan. For Freud, the unconscious isn't a big mess. It's a system. The reason that the things in it have to be kept away from consciousness is because they're deemed unsettling to the person's good image of themselves. Not because they're formless or too qualitatively different to conscious ideas for the two systems to understand one another. They understand each other very well, which is why they are able to keep trying to reach mutually agreeable compromises. There may even be times where they don't have to compromise very much. A repressed wish can suddenly become perfectly allowed if it finds a way to align itself with something ego-syntonic. If your repressed anger at a sibling suddenly finds a cause which you think justifies it, then you can really go to town and take out all your hatred on them.

A very famous example of this sort of shift in values can be found in the story of Lot and his daughters, from Genesis. They've escaped from Sodom and Lot's wife has unfortunately looked back and been turned into a pillar of salt. So Lot and the daughters go and hide in a cave believing that the rest of the world has been destroyed. In order to save humanity they have to seduce their father and have babies with him. The idea which, back in Sodom, would have been totally unacceptable, suddenly becomes a very noble act and they can perform it knowing that they're doing the right thing.

Words and things in the unconscious

I want to say one last thing about Freud's paper before moving on to Lacan. In it there's a section on schizophrenia and displacements due to repression. Freud says you see something very odd happening in schizophrenia and gives two examples. One is a patient of his who can't stop squeezing the blackheads on his nose. He fidgets with his skin and seems to get satisfaction from the eruption of pus. There appears to be something masturbatory about the activity. He gets very upset by the idea that he has ruined his skin by scarring it—that after squeezing a blackhead he is left with a hole. He sees the holes as vaginas—so his masturbatory activity leaves him castrated, with a hole instead of a penis. Freud says that a neurotic person would be unlikely to use a tiny hole in the skin as the symbol for a vagina—it just isn't similar enough. Plus the fact that there are lots of holes makes them an even less obvious choice. While a neurotic may see every medium-sized cavity as an orifice, they would be unlikely to view a multitude of tiny holes in the same way. It's simply the fact that both things can be described using the word "hole" that makes them interchangeable for the patient. Likewise for another patient who sees the little gaps in the knitting of his socks as vaginas and is disturbed by the idea of wanting to unravel them. Again, it's the word that is important in making the connection. In schizophrenia, it appears, words have predominance over things.

Freud describes schizophrenia as a narcissistic disorder. Object-cathexes are given up and the ego is hypercathected, leading to the terrifying loss of reality. The person may become "the one", or they may feel they have to save the world, or that the government/aliens are watching them constantly. But Freud says that, while object-cathexes are given up, word-cathexes aren't. Words might be invested with an overload of excitement, while appearing to be quite free-standing and cut loose from the things they supposedly represent. This leads Freud to say, then, that word-presentations and thing-presentations are not the same, but can be bound together in a secondary operation. And this is where he concludes something about the difference between a conscious and an unconscious presentation. The unconscious contains what he calls "the first and true object-cathexes" (ibid., p. 201), which exist in the unconscious as thing-presentations. The first big excitements are all registered there. The system preconscious comes about as things are linked with words. He talks about thing-presentations being hypercathected through being linked with word-presentations. So this acquisition of language is something quite exciting and there's a big incentive to do it; through it you can organise relations, manage absences and have an effect on the world. At the same time you also learn that certain things have to be given up—you generally become socialised and "realistic" (or you don't …). And becoming socialised involves repression. You have to limit your unacceptable impulses. This is a message you are constantly receiving as you grow up.

The preconscious system is linked with the development of language and with prohibition. The key difference, for Freud at this stage, between an unconscious presentation and a preconscious one is to do with whether or not the cathexis is representable in words. He explains that what repression denies to the object-cathexis is the "translation into words", more particularly "words which shall remain attached to the object" (ibid., p. 202). Unless you express it directly, then it doesn't count. So repression makes an idea unsayable. Even if you were given the words by someone else—someone who knows about psychoanalysis, perhaps, and thinks they know what your unconscious is up to—then the words still wouldn't be attached to the object, they would remain detached from it (even if they were exactly the "right" words). This is why one wouldn't generally make a big interpretation at the beginning of a treatment. It doesn't matter how "correct" it is, you won't be helping the person in any way whatsoever. In fact you will just as likely make them run a mile.

So now that's all perfectly cleared-up and straightforward we can wonder why everyone got into such a mess about it afterwards. Maybe including Freud himself. After Freud made this very serious attempt to be precise about the unconscious it may still have seemed to him to be too complicated or unclear. So a few years later he developed his second model of the mind. Instead of the unconscious, the preconscious, and the conscious you have the id, the ego, and the superego (first outlined in the 1923 book, *The Ego and the Id*). It doesn't replace the old topology, but runs alongside it. You can't say that the id is the unconscious or that consciousness is analogous with the ego, although people sometimes do. Also, maybe it's worth mentioning that the terms we use come from James Strachey's translation. Freud's words in German are Es, Ich, and Über-Ich—it, I and over-I. In German it's much simpler—non-specialist and non-jargony. He's really trying to get his point across in a way that people can understand. But the Strachey translation very possibly added to the confusion: what's the id? A little beast that lives inside you? How are you supposed to think about it? Freud was criticised for almost seeming to personify the various agencies of the mind, creating a kind of mythology.

Freud's book *The Ego and the Id* became very important among certain groups of analysts, namely Anna Freud and the American ego psychologists. There's the big question of what psychoanalysis is for. What kind of a cure is it? For Freud, it seems to have been a problematic one at best, with Dora running off and telling him he was rubbish and the Wolf Man spending the rest of his life saying how little he had helped him. There appears to have been little doubt for Freud about the truth of his findings—the question was what on earth you were supposed to do with it.

The Ego and the Id offers a way to think about cure. The id is unruly and terrible and only wants to do what it wants to do. The superego is made up of every bit of restrictive bossiness the child has incorporated in the course of his development, and the poor old ego sits in between the two fretting about how on earth it's going to cope. So Anna Freud and the ego psychologists further developed this idea to say that the point in psychoanalysis is to help the ego do its job. In her introduction to Freud's essay, Anna Freud explains it like this:

> Thus in every individual, the search for pleasure, for adaptation and for morality clash with each other and over and over confront each of us with the task of reconciling the irreconcilable and, all contradictions notwithstanding, to strive for inner harmony. When these efforts succeed, psychic health is assured; when they fail we see inhibitions, symptoms, and morbidly increased anxiety—pathological manifestations. (1991, p. 436)

You can see from the quote that it's a bit of a mixed bag. Alongside the ideas of inner harmony and psychic health you also have contradiction and irreconcilability. At least mid-twentieth century ego psychology still attempts to take human complexity into account at some level, unlike some of the newer treatments (like CBT) where people are expected to reach inner harmony and integration using a few simple techniques.

Lacan and the unconscious

Here, I want to talk a bit about "The function and field of speech and language in psychoanalysis" (Lacan, 1966, pp. 31–106) where Lacan attacks newer developments in psychoanalysis. But maybe it's useful to start with this famous quote from *Seminar XX*:

> You see that by still preserving this 'like' (comme), I am staying within the bounds of what I put forward when I say that the unconscious is structured like a language. I say like so as not to say—and I come back to this all the time—that the unconscious is structured *by* a language. (1972–1973, p. 48)

You very often hear the middle bit of the quote all by itself, "the unconscious is structured like a language", but here Lacan makes a big point of saying that this doesn't mean that language imposes its rules on the unconscious, or that language creates the unconscious in its image, or whatever other misunderstandings you might be able to pull out of that phrase. So what else might it mean? And especially in relation to Freud's idea that what keeps a thing unconscious is the fact of its being prevented from attaching itself to a word presentation? You'll sometimes read (for instance, on Wikipedia) that, after Freud, Jung and Lacan came up with very different ways of conceiving the unconscious. Jung developed the notion of the collective unconscious, which has been honed in man over generations and which everyone needs to tap into in order to be more at one with the world and with each other. According to Jung, everyone has lodged within them a similar set of unconscious notions that affect the way they interpret the world. On the other hand, according to popular thinking, Lacan came up with the notion of the "linguistic unconscious" which is totally different to Freud's idea. But then you have to ask which of Freud's ideas, because the Lacanian idea isn't anything like this mythical id creature, but it's very much like the unconscious from the first topology. Still, maybe that becomes harder to spot if you say the contents of the Freudian unconscious are barred from attaching themselves to word-presentations, and the Lacanian unconscious is structured like a language. Doesn't it follow then that they must be radically different? Well, not really, given Lacan's insistence on the phrasing, "like a language".

In the Freudian unconscious you have certain phenomena, object-cathexes, that need to be dealt with. If they are deemed too unacceptable to be allowed into consciousness then they need to transform themselves somehow so that the impulse can hope to achieve some sort of satisfaction. The unconscious scouts around for a substitute for the object—something with similar features (for instance, in the case of Little Hans, the father's moustache becomes a horse's noseband). So, ideas or objects are interchangeable, like words. They take on meanings in relation to other words, but there's nothing that says they necessarily have to mean that. Words only take on significance as part of a system, and it's the same with unconscious ideas. As Freud says, in phobia the triggering objects or ideas move further and further away from the central, unacceptable idea. If you have, say, the idea of the sexually desirous father, this becomes the intruder, which becomes the face on the other side of the window, which becomes the curtain covering the window, and so on. Meaning can slip from one object to another. In the same way that green might just as well be called yellow, the intruder might just as well be signified by a curtain, and then the light that illuminates the curtain. But in the unconscious you are always led back to a master signifier, in this case the libidinally invested dad. The master signifier is where the chain stops. So you can see that this is totally different to saying that the unconscious is structured by a language. It's saying that the unconscious is structured according to the same logic as a language.

"The function and field of speech and language in psychoanalysis" (Lacan, 1966, pp. 197–268) is the paper that Lacan gave in Rome in 1953 after he had broken away from the psychoanalytic establishment and formed his own society. He was facing all sorts of problems with other analysts, especially over the question of how to train analysts, and the acceptability of variable length sessions. In the "Rome discourse" he gets extremely worked up about the sorts of things he sees going on in the analytic world. There's his attack on Ernst Kris (an ego psychologist) for mixing up the words "need" and "demand". It's quite vicious. If you read the Kris paper that he's referring to it's hard to agree that what Kris says is really so bad. Kris is actually being self-critical, noticing his initial failure to distinguish the two words and correcting his error. But Lacan refers to this as Kris's "gibberish" (ibid., p. 244). He's very impassioned in his critique. He's been told that what he's doing isn't legitimate or properly in keeping with Freud's legacy. So his "return to Freud" is a kind of cheeky response to that. He's basically saying that he's much more Freudian than all of the post-Freudians, including Freud's daughter (And it's not just Anna Freud and the ego psychologists who get it in the neck—the Kleinians and the British object relations school come in for a battering too).

The question of training analysts is a big one because at the heart of it is the question of what a psychoanalyst is. What are you training people to be or to do? It apparently seemed to Lacan that the object relations people and the American ego psychology people, and the people in France who were beholden to the International Psychoanalytic Association, were heading off in all sorts of wrong directions. The ego psychologists were terrible because they'd gone haring off after this idea that it's possible to achieve a kind of synthesis of the subject through psychoanalysis—Lacan calls it "totality in the individual". Freud had already explained at great length why this was never really going to happen. You might lift the odd repression and ease things up a bit but you're never going to tame your unconscious. Freud spoke about the "navel of the dream" in *The Interpretation of Dreams* (see Freud, 1900a, p. 525). He insisted that there would always be something that you can't quite get at because, no matter how much you might want to be a very clever, psychoanalysed person, you'll always warp your own perceptions and you'll never have a totally clean, clear mind where everything's been given a name and a place and made sense of and controlled. Something will always escape you. According to Freud, human beings are inescapably divided by the unconscious and there's no hope of them achieving mastery over it. If you accept this, then any kind of analysis that involves helping someone to make little bargains between their ego, their conscience, and their craving for pleasure, with the ultimate aim of making everything OK, is fundamentally flawed. The aim of it could only be to interrupt the disruptive force of the unconscious by giving the subject better means to defend against it and to stop it being so pesky. In such a treatment there would be no real need to listen out for the unconscious because the point is to shut it up. Needless to say, this is precisely what many contemporary treatments aim to do.

Then there are the object relations people who are very caught up with the idea of the pre-linguistic, and with looking beyond the surface by treating much of what the patient says as interference, trying to see what's really going on by studying their actions. So before a patient even says anything they might interpret the fact that they are late, suggesting that they don't really want to be there. Or they might tell the patient that they are feeling anxious because there's a break coming up, before the patient has said anything of the sort. There's not such an interest in the particular words the patient uses, or the way in which they use them, there is more of a focus on what the words might be obscuring. Dreams are interpreted in relation to what's going on in the transference rather than in terms of details and fragments, and how these might feature in terms of the subject's unique unconscious lexicon.

So, there are all these problems that are surfacing in psychoanalysis—according to Lacan. There's the idea of a "cure" that dams up the unconscious, there's a mode of interpreting that privileges actions over speech, as if it's only through these that a person gives themselves away. Then there's the Jungian notion that you can have a generally applicable key to unconscious symbols. And on top of all that you have the fact that a general familiarity with Freudian concepts (albeit in a degenerated form) means that people are forewarned against them.

The things that Lacan is arguing for in the "Rome discourse", then, aim at being some kind of antidote to all of that. His return to Freud is a return to the idea of the Freudian unconscious, particularly the way in which it is conceptualised in the 1915 essay. In other words, an unconscious that is constantly pushed to invent its own language or means of articulating itself. An unconscious that replaces a father with a curtain because that's the best means it can find at the time. An unconscious that's totally different in each person.

What does that mean in practice? You have to listen out for the particularities of the patient's language. You have to let your patients make their own associations. You have to take seriously their free-associations and never imagine you know what their dreams mean according to some clichéd ideas about symbolism. So you're trying to hear those odd connections and unlikely rhymes and overlaps. In other words, you're looking out for signs of this language-like unconscious echoing through the person's speech.

References

Freud, A. (1991). *The Essentials of Psycho-Analysis*. London: Penguin [first published London: Hogarth, 1986].

Freud, S. (1895). *Project for a scientific psychology. S. E., 1*: 281–392. London: Hogarth, 1966.
Freud, S. (1898a). *Sexuality in the aetiology of the neuroses. S. E., 3*: 259–285. London: Hogarth, 1962.
Freud, S. (1900a). *The Interpretation of Dreams. S. E., 4–5*. London: Hogarth, 1955.
Freud, S. (1901b). *The Psychopathology of Everyday Life. S. E., 6*. London: Hogarth, 1960.
Freud, S. (1905c). *Jokes and Their Relation to the Unconscious. S. E., 8*. London: Hogarth, 1960.
Freud, S. (1914c). *On narcissism: An introduction. S. E., 14*: 67–102. London: Hogarth, 1957.
Freud, S. (1915e). *The unconscious. S. E., 14*: 159–215. London: Hogarth, 1957.
Freud, S. (1923b). *The Ego and the Id. S. E., 19*: 1–66. London: Hogarth, 1961.
Freud, S. (1940b). *Some elementary lessons in psycho-analysis. S. E., 23*: 279–286. London: Hogarth, 1974.
Freud, S., & Breuer, J. (1895d). *Studies on Hysteria. S. E., 2*. London: Hogarth, 1955.
Jung, C. G. (1912). *On the Psychology of the Unconscious. The Collected Works, 7*: 1–119. London: Routledge and Kegan Paul, 1953.
Lacan, J. (1966). *Écrits*. B. Fink (Trans.). New York: Norton, 2002.
Lacan, J. (1972–1973). *The Seminar of Jacques Lacan. Book XX, Encore*. J. -A. Miller (Ed.), B. Fink (Trans.). New York: Norton, 1999.

CHAPTER TWO

The place of the mirror phase in Lacan's work

Gerry Sullivan

The importance of what the mirror stage (or phase) represents runs through the whole of Lacan's work, from his early, liminally psychoanalytic work on paranoia, to the last phase of his work, where he is searching for a clinical and theoretical strategy consonant with his three registers: the imaginary, the symbolic, and the real being equipotent.

However, if we choose to roughly divide his work into three periods, then the mirror phase provides the emblematic kernel of Lacan's work, from the initial psychiatric focus on paranoia, at the beginning of the 1930s, to the emergence, in the early 1950s, of Lacan's return to the Freud of the first topography, i.e. of the early works of the "talking cure", *The Interpretation of Dreams* (Freud, 1900a), *The Psychopathology of Everyday Life* (Freud, 1901b), and *Jokes and Their Relation to the Unconscious* (Freud, 1905c). We might call it the synthetic apparatus which gives coherence to the orientation which Lacan was taking, over those decades, to the legacy of Freud's work.

Historical context

Although Freud was still alive during the 1930s—the first decade of Lacan's creative work—his legacy had been under active construction since the early 1920s. This had begun in the wake of the panic induced in Freud's close associates by their concern regarding his imminent demise, following the discovery of his mouth cancer in 1923. This led to a much tighter codification of training procedures and the setting up of explicit training institutes, even during the period when Freud himself was revolutionising the theoretical underpinnings of psychoanalysis with the introduction of his second topography, that involved the twin life and death drives, and the agencies of the ego, superego, and the id.

There also followed a gradual drift towards a theoretical orthodoxy over the following decades. Ironically, but understandably, it was the agency of the ego, *das Ich*, from the second topography, which was to prove the focus and organising principle of this evolution.

The agency of the ego was the replacement (with significant modifications), in the second topography, for the function of consciousness in the first topography. The latter function had represented Freud's attempt to specify the unifying effects of the psyche, in its relations with the exigencies of external reality. This approach possessed a certain coherence in the light of Freud's assumption of a distinct separation between pleasure drives, representing demands for satisfaction from internal sources, and ego drives endeavouring to mediate between these demands and the exigencies of external reality. Consciousness may then be held to be the representation of the unity of potential responses to these demands, or, at least, the unity of presentation to the mind of the dilemmas occasioned by the divergent demands.

However, Freud never quite resolved the question of the place of consciousness in his theory. Instead, he faced a growing realisation, rendered explicit in his metapsychological paper "On narcissism" from 1914, that ego drives are irrevocably contaminated with pleasure drives. In particular, the experience of the person as unified, exemplified in the unified self-image, is inseparable from the libidinal investment of this unity.

Furthermore, this is the only pathway towards a substantial measure of a sense of separation between oneself and another person, insofar as libidinal dynamics are involved. The early libidinal dynamics between infant/child and carer involve a libidinal bond based on dependency, an "anaclitic" love bond Freud called it, which precludes an adequate experience of separation between infant/child and carer. The carer is responded to in the form of a more or less adequate extension of the self. It is only in the context of a narcissistic investment of the other that the potential exists, passing through the conflictual aspects of the Oedipal dynamic, for an experience of the separateness of the other to be substantially settled.

With the formulation of the ego as an agency in the second topography, this conception of its functioning as a unifying or mediating agency, irrevocably contaminated with libidinal dynamics, continued, but with the complications introduced by the specification of the other two agencies, the superego and the id. Indeed, we might schematically characterise the subsequent history of mainstream IPA psychoanalysis as variations on the theme of primacy in the ego's relations with the other agencies.

The tradition stemming from the work of Melanie Klein gives primacy to the dynamic of the relation between the ego and the id, as determining the pathway towards a more or less adequate stabilisation of the psyche in its engagement with the buffeting effects upon it of external realities (here we must ally with the id the unconscious, primitive, aggressive aspects of the superego). The various object relations approaches belong in this lineage.

On the other hand, there are the traditions, stemming from, or correlated with, the work of Freud's daughter Anna, which draw upon the ameliorative side of the superego. As Freud presents it, the superego has a prescriptive, judgmental, hectoring and punitive side, the superego "proper". It also presents another face, the aspirational, idealising side, which Freud termed the ego-ideal. It is this aspect which is to the fore in Freud's conception of an exit from the castration complex (completing the effects of the Oedipus complex), where the acceptance of the experience of castration is mediated through the parallel experience of the promise, through identification, of a possible future experience of the satisfaction foregone in the resolution of the complex. Certain historical contingencies determined that this latter framework would have a profound, and in Lacan's view, baneful effect on the mainstream evolution of psychoanalysis from the 1930s onwards.

In the early decades of the existence of psychoanalysis it had been embraced by Freud's followers with a fervour connected with its perceived revolutionary potential with regard to challenging a whole range of orthodoxies with respect to the human condition, from the sovereignty of conscious human reason to the normality of human sexuality with respect to its procreative rationale. We have mentioned the hesitation in this momentum occasioned by the fear of Freud's imminent demise in the early 1920s. As this decade proceeded, and more especially as fascist and anti-Semitic forces became politically and socially potent during the 1930s, this cultural revolutionary ardour faded, and indeed reversed in many, though by no means all, quarters within the psychoanalytic movement.

In the inter-war period psychoanalysis was still largely based in the mainly German speaking lands which had been on the losing side during the First World War. They had consequently suffered both national humiliation and economic hardship, for a variety of reasons. Furthermore, psychoanalysis, especially in relation to its directing forces, remained an overwhelmingly Jewish based movement over these decades. While the remark attributed to Freud, on his first visit to America, that he was bringing a transformative "plague", could be voiced with equanimity before the first world war, by the 1930s it was understandable that much of the psychoanalytic movement was searching for an accommodation with orthodoxy which would act as a shield against the growing vituperative attacks on psychoanalysis as part of a putative vast "Jewish conspiracy" which racial nationalist and fascist forces in Europe saw as threatening to undermine western civilisation. As the centre of gravity of influence within the psychoanalytic movement shifted towards the U.S., the presence of the Jewish Diaspora from Europe, as well as the anti-communism and social conservatism of the U.S. during the 1950s reinforced and, in some measure, extended this effect.

The symptomatic theory of this accommodation with social, cultural, and intellectual orthodoxy was termed "ego psychology" by its initial champions, Kris, Rapaport, and Lacan's analyst Loewenstein. The theoretical basis of the approach related to the notion that there was a normative maturation of the individual which reconciled the said individual to social and biological norms. The therapeutic basis of the approach centred on the functioning of the ego of the analyst as an ideal for the ego of the analysand, whereby "the healthy portion of the ego" of the analysand could enter into a "therapeutic alliance" with that of the analyst, thus guiding the direction of the therapy towards its normative goal (Hartmann, 1939).

Lacan

If we now turn to where Lacan stood in relation to these historical circumstances, the first thing to note is that his background, as the offspring of a solid upper bourgeois French Catholic family, shielded him from the pressures Jewish psychoanalysts faced, even when France was occupied by Germany. Secondly, although professionally Lacan remained a well connected and well respected psychiatrist throughout his life, he was also, from the outset of his career, a cultural radical. He was sympathetic to the surrealist movement from the early 1930s, and indeed, Salvador Dali credited his artistic philosophy of "critical paranoia" to discussions with Lacan.

His post-graduate psychiatric work was on paranoia. Already here he is focusing on the connection between ego and narcissism, with an emphasis which is perhaps more clear-cut than Freud's. Furthermore, using the twin themes of persecution/punishment and grandeur, he specifies that, in cases of "punishment paranoia", the very constitution of the ego is related to the narcissistic dynamic in connection with a privileged other.

This theme is originally advanced in the context of a pathological dynamic. The evolution of Lacan's subsequent thought on this matter mirrors that of Freud, in the latter's pathway towards founding psychoanalysis. We recall that Freud initially located the pathology of hysterical neurosis in the inability of the psyche to process a premature sexual experience into the memory of an event, leading to the later appearance of symptoms memorialising the unremembered event.

In the founding gesture of psychoanalysis proper, Freud universalises the traumatic effect of the human experience of sexuality, by way of the Oedipus complex. Similarly, Lacan universalises the themes he had outlined in his work on paranoia by way of his use of the mirror apparatus, realised in the notion of a mirror phase in the development of the human child.

He had first been alerted to the mirror phenomenon through the writings of his friend, the psychologist Henri Wallon. In his 1934 text, "*Les origins du charactère chez l'enfant*", Wallon had drawn attention to a child developmental phenomenon, previously noted by Charles Darwin and others:

> Darwin notes that toward the eighth month, he manifests with an "Ah!" his surprise each time his look happens to encounter his image, and Preyer notes that at the thirty-fifth week, he eagerly extends his hand towards his image. [...] The reality attributed to the image is in fact so complete that, between the forty-first and forty-fourth week, not only does Preyer's child laugh and extend his arms toward it every time he sees it, but Darwin's child looks at his mirror-image every time he is called by name. When he hears his name, he no longer applies it, albeit in a passing or intermittent fashion, to his proprioceptive self, but rather to the exteroceptive *image* of himself that the mirror offers him. (quoted by Julien, 1994, pp. 29f)

Lacan takes this hint from Wallon and fashions it into a tool with which to clarify Freud's theory of the ego from the second typography.

We have noted that the mainstream IPA analytic traditions have taken the ego, either in its relations to internal objects, or as it relates to projected ideals, as the main focus of their theory and practise. Thus they have concentrated on the inner world of the psyche, the *Innenwelt*, or on the interactions of the psyche with its environment, the *Umwelt*. With the introduction of the mirror apparatus, Lacan locates something new. The ego is now a product of the relationship between the child and the environment. The initial introduction of the mirror apparatus as a developmental phase by Lacan was in a speech given to the 14th IPA Congress at Marienbad, in 1936, but the text of the speech was not published. The earliest published presentation we have is in the 1938 text on "Family complexes" (Lacan, 1938). Here Lacan specifies that the prematurity of human birth, with respect to the maturation of motor and other faculties, creates conditions whereby a womb-like environment, external to the mother's body, must be provided for the child over an extended period. Inevitable perturbations in this provision, as well as the staged withdrawal of aspects of the provision, produce mental drive complexes (the human equivalent of instinctual drives in animals, but whereas the latter are more or less adequate to the achievement of their objects, the extended helplessness of human infants induces attempted hallucinatory satisfactions which catapult the infant into the pleasure principle-reality principle dynamic explored by Freud) whose earliest manifestation Lacan characterises as the "weaning complex". Hence Lacan is pleased to find a confirmation of this general approach as consonant with that of Freud. When the latter's "Project for a scientific psychology" of 1895 is finally published during the 1950s, Lacan notes, in his seminar on *The Ethics of Psychoanalysis* (1959–1960) that, for Freud, the structure of the psyche is a reaction to the effects of overwhelming stimulation on the infantile human organism effected by its primordial helplessness to satisfy its instinctual needs.

For the following complex Lacan borrows a term from Freud, the "fraternal complex", to capture the first stirrings of an independent relation to the other. It is in this context that he introduces the notion of the mirror phase dynamic. First, he notes the probable biological necessity of an anticipation of organic unity embodied in the mirror image, in co-ordinating a movement to such unity. Second, he notes the libidinal jubilation associated with the recognition of the unity of the self presented by way of the mirror image. This aspect of the libidinal investment in the unity of the image permits him to locate the origin of two significant, negatively coloured affects which characterise the relation to the other, the counterpart, in a dyadic dynamic.

The first involves, what is effectively the negative complement of Freud's anaclitic love bond, dependency love. Lacan highlights a remark of Augustine's, in his *Confessions*, which concerns the bitter look, the *invidia conspectu*, which the young child casts at his younger sibling, the milk child, whose suckling at the mother's breast presents a vision of sated unity. As Lacan remarks, it is not that the older child wishes to take the place of the younger. What is unbearable for it is the presentation, in the image, of an unalloyed experience of unity and satiety, from which the weaned, older child is irremediably exiled. This sense of loss Lacan associates with the sentiment of envy, and the reactive tendency to obliterate the intrusive, hated image of unity.

Thus the mirror phase, in introducing the jubilatory experience of unity, also marks it as an anticipated unity, and hence a possibly precarious unity. Lacan points to the play of young children, two-year-olds are mentioned, as exemplifying a solipsistic relation to their little playmates, their counterparts. He notes the processes of parade, travesty, and seduction as typical of the play with a little other, or others, who are experienced as little more than props for the externalised self-affirmation and exploration of the little individual. In this regard, he also notes the ubiquity of the phenomenon of transitivism with this age group, typified by an assault of some kind perpetrated upon a little other, being followed by a reaction such as crying on the part of the perpetrator, indicative of a confusion of identities between the roles of perpetrator and victim. A further extension of this process of the "fraternal complex" involves the emergence of the sentiment of jealousy, the second of the negatively coloured sentiments. Here, the situation that a love object (a loved counterpart) directs his affection towards another (i.e., a third) leads to a rivalrous identification with this other by way of the mirror dynamic. In a sense, for the little one, at this juncture, the rival is as much his ego, as his alter ego. When the resolution of the Oedipal dynamic has tempered the aggressiveness implicit in the mirror dynamic, this original jealousy will transform and become the basis for the affectionate feeling one has for one's fellow human being, one's social counterpart (see Freud's "Group psychology and the analysis of the ego," 1921c).

Hence the elements underpinning the pathology of self punishment paranoia (which Lacan had uncovered in the psychiatric cases of Aimée and the Papin sisters), i.e., the source of the paranoic's ego in the image of another, deemed complete (at the expense of the paranoic subject, with the confusion of identities and the consequent retributive aggression), and he now generalised this understanding into the notion that the ego, in its core nature, has a paranoic structure. It was perhaps the attendance at Kojeve's seminar on Hegel's *Phenomenology of Mind*, during the years in which he was formulating his use of the mirror theme, which emboldened him to make this generalisation. Whatever the case, over subsequent decades, he would interweave themes from Hegel's *Phenomenology* (e.g., the struggle to the death between masters over recognition, "pure prestige"; the master-slave dialectic, distinguishing authorisation and knowledge; the subject as "beautiful soul", determining all discord to which she is subjected, in her innocence, as due to the disorder of the external world) with the ego as a paranoic agency, interpreted through the mirror apparatus, in order to clarify many pathological mechanisms within the psyche.

There is an element implicit in the dynamic of the mirror phase, which will be of importance for the role it will subsequently occupy in Lacan's thought. The recognition of the self-image involved in the mirror dynamic involves a judgement of identity, of identification, which connects it with Freud's notion of the judgement involved in the presentation of an idea, of a *Vorstellung*, to the mind. Lacan developed the connection between recognition, judgement, and logic in his 1946 paper on "Logical time" (*Écrits*, 1966, pp. 161–175). However, the connection between these terms and the mirror dynamic is not developed until the third phase of Lacan's work, from the 1960s onwards. This is because, from the late 1940s onwards, in the second period of his work, Lacan is becoming interested in the role of language as structure, modelled on the discipline of structural linguistics, in throwing light on the nature of the Freudian unconscious, and of unconscious processes. It is in this context that he produces his famous aphorism that the unconscious is structured like a language. From this position he begins to examine Freud's first topography and its cognate texts. He begins to re-read Freud's classic texts in this light. An early example of this is his re-reading of the Rat Man case in his paper "The neurotic's individual myth" (1953), where he highlights the symbolic representatives, in the Rat Man's psyche, of the dilemmas and aporias of love and money of the Rat Man's parents, as constituting the Rat Man's unconscious. The activity of the signifying battery, which these symbolic representatives constitute, is directed towards the resolution, in phantasy, of the legacy left through the aporias of life and love of the previous generation.

In exploring these new areas, the mirror dynamic is re-positioned by Lacan. He now postulates three registers as generating psychic life: the symbolic, the imaginary, and the real. The mirror dynamic is now seen as emblematic of the imaginary. Whereas in the 1930s and 1940s Lacan had emphasised the positive, empowering side of the mirror phase, even in its illusionary nature, in the second phase of his work it is the illusory side, the misapprehension of completion or totality (leading to the illusion of mastery of bodily, especially muscular, functions) which he highlights. He therefore pinpoints two sides of this dynamic. The first concerns the phenomenology of the mirror apparatus, the apprehension of it as an existential phase or stage. He now adds an extra element which subverts the aspect of mastery embodied in the 1930s version. Now the child is held by a caregiver, typically the mother, in front of the mirror. Immediately prior to the joyous and triumphant recognition of the image of the body in the mirror, the child turns to the caregiver, in a gesture which Lacan interprets as soliciting a prerequisite approval, prior to recognition of the image as self-image. Here the caregiver embodies the primacy of the symbolic dimension as anchoring and subtending the mirror dynamic. Hence, secondly, the mirror dynamic as mis-cognition and illusion becomes emblematic of the claims, whether explicit or implicit, to completion and totality, in whatever sphere they are posed. Thus, the motifs crystallised in the mirror apparatus—mastery, unity, totality, and completion—become the characteristic indices of the register of the imaginary, with the judgement that they are mis-cognitions and illusions. In particular, the role ascribed to the ego in Freud's second topography, as the mediating and unifying agency within the psyche, is highlighted by Lacan as exemplary with respect to the illusions underpinning the imaginary register. This being so, Lacan draws the conclusion that the psychic domains underpinned by egoic processes operate in a similar manner.

Hence, the sphere of reality is, in Lacan's view, substantially impregnated with imaginary aspects. He even views it as an extension of dreaming, in so far as both reality and the dream state are complementary modes of avoiding an encounter with the real of trauma. Also, Lacan's elaboration of a theory of the unconscious phantasy, during the second phase of his work, essentially regards it as having the structure of what Freud called the unconscious portion of the ego and hence that of the mirror dynamic. Like the mirror dynamic, Lacan conceives of the phantasy as based on imaginary elements organised around a symbolic element, the phallic signifier, whose effect, in this case, is to effect an imaginary closure, a totality or unity, resisting the gap or lack produced by castration.

At the end of the 1950s, Lacan is beginning to shift the focus of his work away from the Freudian texts, to investigate the place of the object in analytic theory. He offers various optical schemas concerning the place of the object of libidinal investment, which alter his conception of the imaginary to the extent that it is now perceived as potentially embodying a real core. The mirror dynamic now takes on characteristics which might be sketched as follows: while the 1930s mirror scenario emphasised the libidinal investment of the image, with its attendant aspects of unity, agency, and identity, and the jubilation it evokes, there is now the notion of palpable but un-locatable gaps in the image, where libidinal dynamics generate a *frisson* of confused, anticipatory interest, which Lacan characterises in his portrayal of the subjective experience of the analytic object as "nothing, maybe nothing".

In his work of the first half of the 1960s, the place of the object in the visual field is a recurrent theme. However, later in the 1960s a new theme begins to emerge, involving the place of the object in social discourse. Here he isolates four particular discourses, one of which, the analytic discourse, he sees as in the process of possible emergence from the accumulated experience of the practise of psychoanalysis (see *Seminar XVII: The Other Side of Psychoanalysis*, 1969–1970). The central discourse, in many ways the founding discourse, he calls the "discourse of the master". It is in some ways a distillation of Hegel's master-slave dialectic into a combinatory, quasi-mathematical formula, which is part of an ongoing attempt on Lacan's part to specify the structure underlying the myths, Oedipal and others, which Freud used to distil the particularity of analytical experience into generalised communicable form. He introduces the term "matheme", based on the notion of "mytheme", which Levi-Strauss had introduced to specify basic units of myth.

The basic units which Lacan permutes to obtain his four discourses are letters distilled and extracted from the four fundamental concepts of psychoanalysis, which he had explored in his *Seminar XI* (1963–1964). From the concept of the unconscious is extracted its subject, a divided subject, ciphered in the letter "$"; from the drive is extracted its ungraspable object, ciphered in the letter "a"; from the concept of transference love is extracted the knowledge imputed to the analyst, as a "subject-supposed-to-know", ciphered in the letter "S"; and finally, from the concept of repetition is extracted the element which repeats, ciphered in the letter "S_1". This S_1 Lacan terms the "master signifier". These four letters are permuted among four places. These places locate the distinct guises under which psychoanalysis encounters the body: as truth, as agent, as Other, and in its paradoxical and unsatisfiable relation to enjoyment.

It is in the discourse of the master that we again encounter the themes that we have isolated from the mirror dynamic. Lacan, with respect to this discourse, associates the agency of the body with what he calls a "semblant", a semblance or seemingness. This seemingness relates to the agency of an S_1, a master signifier. As he explores the role of this signifier, he is led to consider that in order to have a signifier [*un signifier*] there must be the possibility of one signifier where the one evokes a unity, ranging from the individual unity (or atomic indivisibility) of an entity, to the conglomerate unity of a totality. In this discourse also, there is a push towards knowledge, insisting as an enigmatic or equivalent truth emanating from the body which the seemingness of the master signifier is unable to exhaust.

Hence, Lacan introduces the postulant "*il y a de l'Un*", there is something of (the) one, to capture both the necessity, and the existential fragility of these themes of identity, totality, and unity (see *Seminar XIX: ... ou pire*, 1971–1972). In reflecting on the implications of this, over a number of years, Lacan is able to formulate the logic of the masculine side of his formulae of sexuation, in a paradoxical conjoining of the conglomerate totality of the all, with the individual particularity of an exception (see Lacan, 1973). The seeming paradox of this evolution of Lacan's work, in three phases, from the late 1930s to the beginning of the 1970s, is that it culminates in an intrication, rather than a further distinction, between the realms of the symbolic, centred on signifier and structure, and that of the imaginary, whose emblematic motive is the mirror. The masculine side of his formulae of sexuation is his way of extracting a logical structure from Freud's myth of the primal father. As such, it appears to deflate the imaginary elements associated with Freud's myth, the story of the primal horde, the unbridled potency of the primal father, and the fear-filled impotence of the sons. However, in so doing, the central motifs associated with the mirror dynamic from the outset are retained, and indeed clarified. Perhaps the simplest way of illustrating this is to return to Freud. In his book on *Group psychology* (Freud, 1921c) Freud emphasises that the psyche is comprised of a group psychology alongside that of an individual psychology. The structure of social institutions and the organisation of an individual's group psychology are homologous. The grounds of this homology are the functioning of a symbolic element which is both an exception and an ideal.

This is what the structure of the totem and taboo myth conveys (see Freud, 1912–1913). It is also what the mirror phase communicates. As Lacan emphasised from the outset, the unity in the mirror is as much, if not much more, a potential as a reality. The tension between these two he will examine during the 1950s in the form of the discordant link between the ideal ego and the ego-ideal. The post-Oedipal ego is then the agency of negotiation between these two. By the early 1970s this is re-posed in terms of the status of the relationship between the subjection of each one to the unity of an all, and the limiting of this universe of an all, through the existence of an "at least one" not subjected to this all, and therefore an exception. As Lacan has noted, Freud discovered in his clinical work that the omnipresent factor in the psyche of neurotics, which indicated their relationship to potency and identity, could be perfectly ciphered in the ancient symbol of the phallus. At the outset of Lacan's psychoanalytic career in the 1930s, the mirror phase theme fulfils the role of an apparatus through which he can examine the dilemmas of phallic narcissism. Towards the end of his career, he reduces the phallus to being a symbolic term, subject to logical operators in a transformation of the Aristotelian logical square. Nevertheless, as we have emphasised, it is the same dilemmas of the human subject that are highlighted, those concerning agency, unity, totality, and identity.

Conclusion

In his *Seminar XI* of 1973–1974, Lacan re-iterates that the question of the mirror continues to resonate in his work. However, we have mentioned in passing that the effect of the libidinal object, according to Lacan, is to produce a hole in the mirror image. During the period when he was developing his theory of the psychoanalytic object, the *petit objet a*, he produced a series of complex optical schemas elaborated from the original mirror phase schema. We have not followed this thread in Lacan's work, in this introductory sketch, for a very particular reason. In Lacan's schema L, from the 1950s, the imaginary register is ciphered in the line "a'-a", a distillation into algebraic form of the mirror relation between the individual human being and his counterpart (see Lacan, "*Seminar on 'The Purloined Letter'*", in: *Écrits*, 1966, p. 40). Through a series of stages there gradually emerged a distinct, but parallel dyad to that of a'-a. This is the relation between $, the human subject as irrevocably divided, and a, now understood as that which is unrepresentable in any register of human subjective experience, from a psychoanalytic perspective. This gives us the glyph, the writing $ ◊ a; capturing the unconscious phantasy as a formal writing, it indicates the possibility of a transcending of the ethic underpinning the myth-based theoretical core of the Freudian clinic. In this sense it acts as the colophon of possibility in relation to the ethic of a post-Freudian clinic.

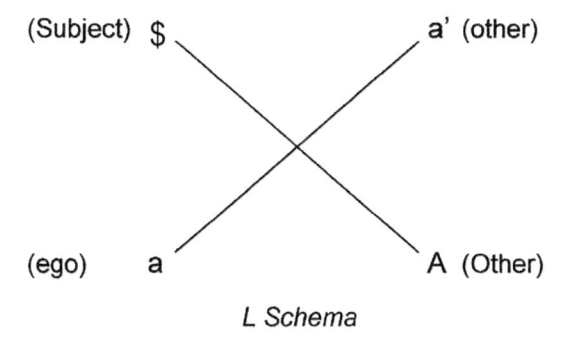

(Subject) $ a' (other)

(ego)   a   A (Other)

L Schema

Nevertheless, it continues to exist substantially on the level of possibility. This is one interpretation of Lacan's remark during the 1970s that while his followers might consider themselves Lacanian's, he remained a Freudian.

Using Lacan's language, we might consider that the aims of a Freudian clinic involve the attenuation or reduction of ideals, and the installation of mechanisms of impossibility, this latter effecting the containing and stabilising of series, by way of limits (as such, it is the formalising of the notion of castration).

All of this is compatible with the masculine side of Lacan's formulae of sexuation. As we have indicated, this chimes with the themes associated with the mirror dynamic from the outset. The other side of the formulae of sexuation, the feminine side, leads us in directions beyond the mirror dynamic, as we have outlined it.

References

Freud, S. (1895). *Project for a scientific psychology. S. E.*, 1: 281–392. London: Hogarth, 1966.
Freud, S. (1900a). *The Interpretation of Dreams. S. E.*, 4–5. London: Hogarth, 1955.
Freud, S. (1901b). *The Psychopathology of Everyday Life. S. E.*, 6. London: Hogarth, 1960.
Freud, S. (1905c). *Jokes and Their Relation to the Unconscious. S. E.*, 8. London: Hogarth, 1960.
Freud, S. (1912–1913). *Totem and taboo. S. E.*, 13: vii–162. London: Hogarth, 1953.
Freud, S. (1914c). *On narcissism: An introduction. S. E.*, 14: 67–102. London: Hogarth, 1957.
Freud, S. (1921c). *Group psychology and the analysis of the ego. S. E.*, 18: 65–143. London: Hogarth, 1955.
Hartmann, H. (1939). *Ego Psychology and the Problem of Adaptation.* D. Rapaport (Trans.). New York: International University Press.
Julien, P. (1994). *Jacques Lacan's Return to Freud.* D. Beck Simiu (Trans.). New York: New York University Press.
Lacan, J. (1938). *Les Complexes familiaux dans la formation de l'individu.* J. -A. Miller (Ed.). Paris: Navarin, 1984.
Lacan, J. (1953). The neurotic's individual myth. M. N. Evans (Trans.). *Psychoanalytic Quarterly, 1979, 48*: 386–425.

Lacan, J. (1959–1960). *The Seminar of Jacques Lacan, Book VII, The Ethics of Psychoanalysis*. J. -A. Miller (Ed.), D. Porter (Trans.). New York: Norton, 1992.

Lacan, J. (1963–1964). *The Seminar of Jacques Lacan, Book XI, The Four Fundamental Concepts of Psychoanalysis*. J. -A. Miller (Ed.), A. Sheridan (Trans.). London: Hogarth, 1977.

Lacan, J. (1966). *Écrits*. B. Fink (Trans.). New York and London: Norton, 2002.

Lacan, J. (1969–1970). *The Seminar of Jacques Lacan, Book XVII, The Other Side of Psychoanalysis*. J. -A. Miller (Ed.), R. Grigg (Trans.). New York: Norton, 2007.

Lacan, J. (1971–1972). *Le Séminaire, Livre XIX, ... ou pire*. J. -A. Miller (Ed.). Paris: Seuil, 2011.

Lacan, J. (1973). L'étourdit. *Scilicet, 1973, 4*: 5–52.

Lacan, J. (1973–1974). *Le Séminaire, Livre XXI, Les non-dupes errent* [unpublished].

Wallon, H. (1934). *Les origines du charactère chez l'enfant*. Paris: Boivin.

CHAPTER THREE

The object from Freud to Lacan

Noga Wine

Lacan's return to the Freudian question of the object led to the introduction of his most important invention: the concept of object *a*. This innovation revitalised his approach to the structure of the subject and consequently both psychoanalytic theory and practice could move beyond the Freudian rock of castration.

The effects of this development, which created a new concept of lack, could be compared to the consequences of the invention of zero in the field of mathematics. Robert Kaplan in his book *The Nothing That Is: A Natural History of Zero*, says: "If you look at zero you see nothing; but look through it and you will see the world. For zero brings into focus the great organic sprawl of mathematics." (1999, p. 1). We could paraphrase Kaplan's observation and say that if you look at object *a*, you see a nothing; but look through it and you will see the structure of the subject, and the principle of the efficacy of psychoanalytic practice.

Zero may be nothing, but when zero is activated in conjunction with other numbers it becomes something. Shakespeare called zero "an O without a figure" (1959, *King Lear*, Act I, Scene IV: 212, p. 915), yet when zero is counted as a figure marking an empty place it becomes very productive in mathematics. If zero began as a mark of an empty place, it gradually started to be articulated with other numbers until it became recognised as a number itself. Object *a* is analogous to zero in this sense: it has no imaginary figuration, yet when it takes on a symbolic denotation as a letter it can interact with other signifiers and generate far reaching results.

We could illustrate the advantages of using zero with the simple example of the basic operation of addition. If we take a system without zero like the roman algorithms and try to add with them, it becomes evident to what extent the decimal system, which has a zero, is more efficient:

47
+
26
=
73

It is quick and clear that we have to move one group of ten units from the unit column to the tens column. But if we try to do this simple calculation with Roman characters it becomes much more complicated because the groupings are not arranged around an empty place:

XLVII
+
XXVI
=
LXXIII

Freud's definition of the object in psychoanalysis

In order to shed some light on the concept of object *a*, we will follow the progression suggested by Vinicius Darriba from Brazil, articulating some of Lacan's steps towards this most remarkable new signifier (Darriba, 2005).

A milestone in the development of Freud's concept of the drives are the "Three essays on the theory of sexuality" from 1905, where "drive" is used as a term and not yet as a concept. Freud remarks that the object is not the most evident element in the drive: "Under a great number of conditions and in surprisingly numerous individuals, *the nature and importance of the sexual object recedes into the background*. What is essential and constant in the sexual drive is *something else*." (1905d, p. 149; my italics)

Later, in 1915, when Freud does construct and define the concept of the drive he says: "The object [*Objekt*] of an instinct [a drive] is the thing in regard to which or through which the instinct [drive] is able to achieve its aim. It is what is *most variable* about an instinct [drive] and is *not originally connected with it*, but becomes assigned to it only in consequence of being peculiarly fitted to make satisfaction possible." (1915c, p. 122; my italics)

At this stage, in the context of the first theory of the drives, the satisfaction of the drive was determined by the aim of attaining pleasure or rather of avoiding displeasure. In the twenties, Freud was compelled to elaborate a second theory of the drives because the aim proved to be more complex than the maintenance of the pleasure principle. His practice made him realise that the drive pushes the subject beyond the pleasure principle. To account for this drive which transgresses any limit of pleasure and good, Freud created his most uncanny concept: the death drive.

Lacan introduced his concept of object *a* in order to bring together Freud's two theories of the drives. He emphasised the lack of an original object for the drive and took into account the "real", the psychoanalytic register which repeatedly goes beyond the pleasure principle. He articulated the variability and lack of determination, that is, the fact that the object is not originally connected to the drive, with the question that motivated Freud to create the second theory of the drives: the compulsion to repeat painful situations. The death drive is a concept introduced in order to account for the compulsion to repeat. As Lacan linked the two theories of the drives, he argued that the compulsion to repeat is caused by the fact that the object is not originally connected to the drive. The primary lack of an object is the ultimate cause of repetition. The drive does not know what it wants, it does not have any knowledge of the object, and desire emerges in order to try to offer some answers to that open question of the drive. Desire will push the subject to craft objects, and these objects that it finds or creates will ease the constant pressure of the drive and give it partial satisfaction, but they will never be able to tame this constant pressure of the drive completely. Thus the subject will be driven constantly from one object to another and his desire will slide between the signifiers of the symbolic order.

Lacan's Seminar IV: *moving from object relations to the relation to lack*

In 1956–1957, Lacan gave a seminar on the theme of "object relations", although he immediately criticised the term object relation itself. He chose that term because it occupied a central position in the theoretical and practical work of the psychoanalytic community at that time. Lacan indicated that his polemic targeted contemporary authors and especially Maurice Bouvet, the president of the *Société psychanalytique de Paris*, which Lacan had left in 1953 (see Razavet, 2000).

In post-Freudian psychoanalytic texts, we find a tendency to substitute the notion of object relation for that of "phase". Abraham emphasised the notion of object relation and subsequently it came to occupy a central place in Melanie Klein's theory. Lacan's criticism refers probably to the content of the article on object relations which Bouvet had published (Bouvet, 1956). Lacan disapproved of the use of this term by the post-Freudians, given that Freud himself was not especially concerned with it, as he spoke of object choice and not of object relations.

The phases of the organisation of the libido

The notion of libidinal phase designates a phase of sexual development of the child characterised by a particular organisation of the libido, governed either by the predominance of one erotogenic zone or by a certain mode of relation or interaction with the object. Later it becomes clear that the notion of phase implies a kind of relation of the subject with his world. Thus an erotogenic zone and a mode of object relating could not be separated.

To start with, Freud distinguished two phases of "pre-genital organisation": one is the oral and the second is the anal-sadistic phase. Only in 1923 in the article "The infantile genital organisation" did he add a third pre-genital organisation called the *phallic phase* (Freud, 1923e, p. 141). In the *phallic phase*, only one genital is recognised: the male one. This phase is dominated by the castration complex and corresponds to the decline of the Oedipus complex. The other sex is not taken into consideration by young children and the female genitals are ignored.

In the *oral phase* the source of the drive is the mouth, the object is the breast, and the aim is the incorporation of the object. The mode of relation here is incorporation and this pre-genital sexual organisation of this phase was called cannibalistic.

The *anal phase* is governed by the anal zone and the mode of relation with the object is active and manifested as a drive for domination. It is characterised by the activity of giving and receiving linked to the expulsion and retention of faeces.

In the *phallic phase* the genitals become the important erotogenic zone. A convergence of the sexual impulses onto the sexual object is realised only to a certain degree. However, as Freud argues, only one genital organ is recognised by children and the opposition between the two genders is characterised by castration: one sex is the phallic one and the other is the castrated. One gender has it while the other does not have it.

The importance of this third phase is that it is connected to the decline of the Oedipus complex. Lacan's whole conception of the ascent of the subject to the symbolic order is grounded on this phase. The relation to the phallus as signifier determines the position of the subject vis-à-vis the symbolic order.

Freud analysed genital sexuality in the essay "The transformations of puberty" (Freud, 1905d, pp. 207–230). He postulated that the new sexual aim of this phase is the discharge of the sexual secretions. Hence, it seems that he subordinated the sexual drive to the function of reproduction. At this stage the obtaining of pleasure converges with the objective of preservation of the species and the sexual drive becomes altruistic. As Freud still seems to subjugate the sexual drive to the reproductive function, the post-Freudians mistakenly reduced the psychoanalytic conception of the drive to a biological one, and this reduction gave rise to the crucial practical and theoretical deviations of object relations theories.

In his return to Freud, Lacan insisted that the apparent ambiguity of the "Three essays on the theory of sexuality" was corrected in 1915 when Freud wrote that the only aim of the drive is satisfaction and that all his following reasoning is based on conceptions of non-totality and lack of harmony, which were introduced into Western thinking along with Einstein's theories of relativity.

Only after Lacan returned to the study of the Freudian concept of the drive was it reinstituted as the major concept of the psychoanalytic field. It is this concept which gives the reason and the cause of the unconscious itself. Indeed, the most important intervention Lacan made in his return to Freud takes place via the problematic of the drive's object. One of the fundamental traits of the drive is its articulation with the object as a lacking object. Although the object is one of the four elements which comprise the concept of the drive, the object of the drive is not predetermined and is not inscribed in the knowledge of the subject's body or mind. Thus, the mental apparatus emerges and develops in order to create or find objects and to offer them to the drive so as to discharge its tension, satisfy it and appease it. The subject will produce something where there was nothing. The whole mental apparatus is driven by the search for the lacking object in an attempt to satisfy a drive which has no innate knowledge of what it desires.

This new perspective makes a crucial difference to clinical orientation. Those theories of object relations which Lacan attacked led to serious clinical divergences because of their concept of the object. They presupposed a harmonic relation between the subject and the object, contrary to Freud's teaching. Lacan reminds us in *Seminar IV* time and again that Freud had warned that the object is the *most variable* element of the drive, with the emphasis on "variable". There is no object which is predestined and predetermined to satisfy the drive, and the essence of the object resides in its variations. There is no ultimate object onto which all the partial drives would converge and in relation to which all the phases of development achieve maturation and harmony. Lacan shows that it is precisely the genital object which renders the lack observable to the little subject and that it is not the object of convergence and totality. For many object relations theorists, the subject would outgrow the pre-genital stages on a developmental route ending in normality and maturity.

Such conceptions of a convergence onto a genital object also presuppose the idea of the maturation of the subject in relation to reality. The genital object would situate the subject in a normative reality and consequently clinical work would aspire to an adaptation to such a reality. Oriented by this so-called adaptation of the subject, the object relations analyst becomes a model and occupies the place of an ideal to be attained.

Lacan shows how the idea that analysis aims at a "maturation" of the subject in relation to reality is misguided. For him, behind any reality the real insists and produces differentiations. He stresses that the human subject is always a subject of desire, a divided subject, lacking both a full identity and a unity. During the whole of *Seminar IV*, Lacan contests the models of objects conceived by object relations theorists, and he insists that the object in Freudian theory refers to a lack. He studies the subject's relation to the lack in three fundamental modalities: privation, frustration, and castration.

This led him to formulate the lack of an object as an object of lack. From 1956 on, he was working towards the creation of his singular object: object *a*. It will no longer be the Freudian lacking object but the object of lack. Putting in place a concept that encompasses the lack, his theory would rule out any confusion of the object with the genital object, and Lacan would make it clear that psychoanalytic theory does not admit any notion of an adequate object in a harmonic relation with the subject. Indeed, years later, in *Seminar XX*, Lacan will coin the famous aphorism that "there's no such thing as a sexual relationship" (1972–1973, p. 12). The concept of object which he will introduce does not guarantee stability, harmony, or homeostasis; on the contrary, it causes an ever-moving and changing desire. Lacan takes desire to be the essence of the human subject, and in the seminars following the seminar on object relations he will focus on the theme of desire.

On the path towards the invention of object *a*, some points from *Seminar VII* are crucial.

Seminar VII: *from the lack to the Thing*

In *Seminar IV*, Lacan had subverted the concept of object relations and stressed the modalities of the subject's relation to the lack of an object: privation, frustration, and castration. In 1959–1960, the theme of Lacan's seminar was the ethics of psychoanalysis. The result of this work was another subversion. Lacan argues that the ethics of psychoanalysis is the ethics of desire. In this new approach to lack, his notion of *das Ding* (the Thing) was central.

The Thing provides a new perspective on the theme of desire. At this point, Lacan's return to Freud involves a kind of return of the repressed. He retrieves a signifier that was "repressed" by Freud, as he had never allowed the "Project for a scientific psychology" from 1895 to be published. However, Lacan found in this manuscript a master signifier that would allow a re-interpretation of the whole of Freud's writings. It is especially fertile for the understanding of that part of Freud's work which was left undeveloped due to its difficulty, the second theory of the drives where Freud introduces the concept of the death drive.

Ethics was traditionally linked to the distinction between what is related to pleasure and what is related to a final or supreme good implied in moral agency. Lacan articulated the distinction between pleasure and good with a discussion of the relation between pleasure and reality, and in this context he focuses on the notion of *das Ding* from the "Project". Freud used the term in Section 16, on "Cognition and reproductive thought", and then in Section 17, on "Remembering and judging" (1895, p. 328, 331). He studied the relation between perception and memory and divided the perceptive complexes into two components. One is a component which could not be assimilated by thought—a *Ding*—and the other is known to the ego through its own experience of movement and it can be retained in memory. As to the part which is not assimilated, Freud claimed that at the level of the *Vorstellungen* (representations) something remains which is included though not assimilated. It is excluded from the psychical organisation. *Das Ding* remains as an excluded interior around which the psychical organisation takes place. Thus, *das Ding* designates an unencompassable aspect of every representation. (That is the neurone *a* which seemed to be identical in perception and in memory, where identity and stability are assumed.) *Das Ding* is an ungraspable centre of gravity that would lend coherence to the various manifestations of an object while remaining itself ineluctably out of reach. One of the most essential functions of the psychical apparatus is to establish identity between the image in memory and the image which comes from perception and to verify a correlation between the two. But there is always something that escapes a perfect coincidence and flawless identity therefore fails. Freud locates the function of *das Ding* in the space of this failure.

The process by which identity is sought, according to Freud, is judgement and "what we call *Things* are residues which evade being judged" (1895, p. 334). Such non-coincidence and the existence of an inassimilable reminder in the form of the Thing is what puts the mind to work. The failed encounter between memory and perception provides the motive for judgement and thought. In Freud's words: "Their non-coincidence gives the impetus for the activity of thought, which is terminated once more with their coincidence" (ibid., p. 328).

Before Lacan approached the object through *das Ding*, the idea that the object was lacking was formulated using the notion of the lost object, implying that it did exist. Now the order is inverted. The loss is not deemed to be the reason for the encounter with an object but, on the contrary, it is an encounter which generates the idea that it is a re-finding of something that had been lost. In the first conception, the idea of the lost object links desire to the re-edition of an experience where that object would have been present, and the lack is referred merely to the permanent failure to find that lost object. Thus the lack of object still remains associated to a supposed empirical origin of desire. When Lacan borrows the notion of *das Ding* from Freud's "Project", however, he is seeking a foundation and a structure for the idea that the lack does not refer to any empirical lost object; instead, it refers to the very condition which makes desire possible. Following this line of thought, Lacan criticises the tendencies of some psychoanalysts to treat the mother as occupying the place of *das Ding*.

In the seminar on object relations, Lacan had already criticised the way the term "frustration" was used by the object relations psychoanalysts and he returned to it in *Seminar VII*. He noted that *das Ding* indicates a primary lack and that this fact is obscured if one restricts the question of object relations to the context of the mother/baby interaction. The lack does not relate to a primordial object; it is this lack (of identity which was glossed over) itself which is at the origin of the experience of desire. The lack is the condition and the cause of desire and it is not the result of any frustration brought about by the mother. In fact, *das Ding* is central as an indication, or the manifestation, of an exterior. If we want to speak about this peculiar topology of *das Ding* we need to tie together in a curious knot that which is central and that which is exterior. Lacan used the term "extimacy" to designate this knot.

The context in which *das Ding* is both interior and exterior is that of the network of signifiers. Lacan relates the Freudian *Vorstellungen* (representations) to the signifiers with which he was working at that point, and affirms that the *Vorstellungen* modulate themselves according to the laws which regulate the functioning of the chain of signifiers. In the "Project", Freud conceives of desire as desire for an object at the level of the *Vorstellungen*, which means that the desire for the object slides along the chain of the signifiers, at the level of language and of the symbolic order. Freud's terms in the "Project" for the symbolic are "thought" and "judgement". *Das Ding* is an exterior centre of the subject of the unconscious, a subject organised by chains of signifiers. In Lacan's terms, it is the real which is afflicted by the signifier. He also calls it the exterior to the signified. Lacan's orientation makes the Freudian Thing a support of what he himself calls the real, that which is inaccessible to language, although it is the condition and effective motor that drives language.

Lacan would also add the term of the "law of language" to the idea of *das Ding*. The Thing is what is separated from everything, so that the subject can start to name objects and articulate them as signifiers. Language can only emerge once the Thing is defined as inaccessible, and so the symbolic law is established as a law which prohibits access to the Thing. It is the law which marks the presence of the real and which puts limits to any total and stable satisfaction of the drive, forbidding full *jouissance*. Total *jouissance*, which designates what would have been achieved through access to the Thing, is made impossible by symbolic law. We could find this idea already in the terms of the "Project" from 1895. Not all the energies which invade the neurones could be discharged, and some would be retained in certain groups of neurones in order to enable the psychical apparatus to emerge and thus system ψ (psychical) differentiates itself from the neurones of system φ (physiological).

From the investigation of *das Ding*, Lacan maps out an inaccessible object, moving towards a concept of an object which will be closely linked to this definition. He wants to conceptualise an object which evokes the substantial lack of *das Ding*. As always, this effort is not purely theoretical and it is firmly grounded in his clinical work.

If Lacan would have ended his elaboration of the object with *das Ding*, it would have perhaps implied a lack which was excluded from psychoanalytic experience. But he wanted to create a conceptual tool that would allow for the effect of exclusion from the network of signifiers to be articulated with the question of the subject and his desire. The inaccessibility of *das Ding* and the prohibition of a full *jouissance* would open a passage to the experience of desire as it is unravelled in the structure of language, along the chains of signifiers. Lacan needed the conceptualisation of the object *a* that included both the trace of *das Ding* and the idea of an object in desire. Theorising this did not entail the total exclusion of *das Ding*, and its traces left a mark like that of a notation of zero.

Das Ding *and sublimation*

In 1959, still during *Seminar VII* on *Ethics*, Lacan arrived at another important milestone on the way towards his invention of object *a*. He articulates the way in which the object is marked by the exclusion of *das Ding*. Again he intervenes by a return to a gap in Freud's writings. Freud had never published his promised metapsychological article on sublimation, and Lacan set about to try and define it. He now gave his famous definition: sublimation elevates the object "to the dignity of the Thing" (Lacan, 1959–1960, p. 112). In this definition, the ultimate destiny of the drive links the object to *das Ding*. His elaboration around the

Freudian *Ding* suggests a found object that was never really lost, and this paradox would open up the question of repetition and of what it is that repeats if there was nothing there in the first place. Lacan suggests that as *das Ding* itself cannot be represented, it will always be represented as "another thing" or "something else", to use Freud's words. The object is already different from the Thing, and each object which represents *das Ding* will represent it by means of *difference itself*. Its being different each time is its very essence, and it will appear each time as a new creation. This "otherness" is the trace of *das Ding* which marks any object with the original lack. The void is represented here as a difference. Thus the object of desire always moves on to another object. No empirical object could fill in the place of *das Ding*, as there is no possibility to fill the void it has left. It is the movement from one object to another which indicates *das Ding* as an exterior motor which motivates the change from one to the other. As Lacan puts it:

> I referred last time to the schematic example of the vase, so as to allow you to grasp where the Thing is situated in the relationship that places man in the mediation function between the real and the signifier. This Thing, all forms of which created by man belong to the sphere of sublimation, this Thing will always be represented by emptiness, precisely because it cannot be represented by anything else—or, more exactly, because it can only be represented by *something else*. But in every form of sublimation, emptiness is determinative. (1959–1960, pp. 129f; my italics)

As the object takes on this character of movement, of difference, of being other, it can become embodied in the empirical sphere, in experience, as a repeating lack and return of the void. Something which was impalpable and intangible becomes, through the analytic experience, a source of creation of "something else", and this will represent *das Ding* as object *a*.

From Freud's compulsion to repeat to Lacan's concept of repetition

In *Seminar XI* (1963–1964) the elaboration around the Thing as inaccessible and as a forbidden satisfaction changed and Lacan approached the theme through the concept of repetition. From the start he had associated *das Ding* with the register of the real. Now the real is conceived in terms of a repetition or a return. The real is defined as that which always returns to the same place. The place is the limit of the symbolic and the imaginary registers. The concept of repetition allows the real and the symbolic to intersect and the real is no longer a pure exteriority. Lacan developed the theme of repetition by borrowing from Aristotle the tension between *automaton* and *tuché*. Repetition in the network of signifiers is at the level of *automaton* and the encounter with the real is *tuché*. Lacan indicated that beyond the repetitive insistence of signifiers, the real persists and reappears at the limit of the chain of signifiers. It is felt as an encounter with the void. Thus, in psychoanalysis, repetition is not conceived simply as the emergence of signifiers which excludes the real, but also as a repetition at the boundary of signifiers, where the real returns as an encounter with the fault or the lack of signifiers or images. It is always a failed or missed encounter.

By 1964, Lacan had consolidated his central thesis on the unconscious. It is structured like a language and consists of a net of signifiers. With the new developments around repetition in *Seminar XI* (Lacan, 1963–1964), Lacan could grasp another aspect of the unconscious: the unconscious as discontinuity. It stumbles on the real, as Freud had shown in "Beyond the Pleasure Principle" (1920g). Lacan concentrated now on the problematic of discontinuity which the unconscious presents, and shifted his attention from the core of the circuits of signifiers to their edges and limits. He argued that it is necessary to go further with the investigation of the Freudian unconscious, and consider the unconscious at the points where it encounters the drive. At the start of *Seminar XI*, Lacan described the unconscious in new terms. Until then it had been described as an order, as a chain with a certain stability, now he puts the emphasis on discontinuity. The unconscious becomes an edge or border, which opens and closes. Thus the unconscious has the characteristics of the erotogenic zone, the source of the drive, and Lacan noted this common element where the symbolic, the unconscious and the mode of functioning of the drive converge. The real and the order of the signifier implicate and affect each other. Lacan indicated in this seminar that the real is the greatest "accomplice of the drive" (Lacan, 1963–1964, p. 69).

In Lacan's first formulation, the analytic experience was conceived in terms of the logic of the web of signifiers. The signifier was the cause of the subject and these signifiers depended on the exclusion of *das*

Ding, which was totally exterior, something which experience could not assimilate. When Lacan introduced the concept of object *a*, he made a new departure. The unconscious was no longer a logic governed by an unassimilated exterior, since the exterior was experienced by the subject and caused effects. The remainder left over from the agency of the signifier did not refer to something transcendent but to something which returned as the cause of experience.

The object now has lack as its very substance. Lacan started by emphasising the lack of the object, then moved to *das Ding*, and subsequently arrived at the object of lack. Object *a* is not conceived as an empirical object which could be assimilated by experience. However, contrary to *das Ding*, it does not designate a pure negativity in experience: on the contrary, the subject of desire experiences object *a* as a cause of desire. It is experienced by the subject as a new edition of the lack of the real thing. Lacan always insisted that *das Ding* means that lack itself has to be situated at the origin; the origin is not any original experience of an object in relation to which the lack would be felt retrospectively. When Lacan invented the concept of object *a*, even the original and primary moment is put into question, given that lack has a synchronic relation to the experience of the object. This means that there is no origin except what is experienced with every new encounter with the object. This is the meaning of an object of lack.

Object a: *in theory and in practice*

The terms *das Ding*, the real and *jouissance* were already linked to the question of lack in the Lacanian discourse. With the concept object *a*, lack is not merely designated but the experience of lack is touched upon. Analytic theory has at its centre an experience of lack, and that experience is its very essence. That is why Lacan said in *Radiophonie* (1970) that object *a* is only deducible in the particular analysis of each subject.

The concept of object *a* testifies to the effort Lacan made to ensure that psychoanalytic theory would focus on the opening of the unconscious. He observed that discontinuity is a dimension necessary to animate the experience which Freud inaugurated. It was thus necessary to give a key place to a concept which would not allow its closure, which would not suture this gap, a concept which, ultimately, would situate itself in this breach. Object *a* implies that the real could not be silenced, would not be forever wordless or speechless. It would be heard in every opening between two signifiers and made to generate new signifiers in a new kind of speech. Thus psychoanalysis offers the potential of permanent reinvention and recreation.

The analyst is now required to occupy the place of object *a*. Indeed, we saw this concept emerge as *agalma* in the theory of transference, very soon after Lacan had introduced the concept of object *a*. Since the seminar on transference (Lacan, 1960–1961) he already thought of the function and the place of the analyst in terms of *agalma*. In *Seminar XI*, he argued that object *a* is the cause of transference (Lacan, 1963–1964, pp. 133f). Later in *Seminar XVII* (1969–1970), he invented the "discourse of the analyst" where object *a* is the agent and the efficient cause in that form of social bond. The analyst will occupy the place of the cause of desire for the analysand.

Object *a* is an attempt to answer the question of the relation between the concept and the lack in psychoanalysis. A concept does not mean a complete and circumscribed theory, but rather a way of keeping the theory alive, open to whatever emerges in analytic practice.

We can now return to the beginning, to Freud's 1895 "Project", and find that the gap, the lack, the impossible ultimate satisfaction of the drive were already there at the start (developed in Wine, 1992). The re-found signifier/object was reanimated by Lacan. We saw how the first theorem of the "Project" already included within it the prohibition of complete *jouissance* together with the wish to attain it. This paradox of the drive emerges from the energetic aspect of the development of the psychical apparatus. The drives put a constant demand on the psychical apparatus and the latter evolves on condition that those demands are only partially met. Freud:

> 1 (a) First principal theorem: The quantitative conception
>
> This is derived directly from pathological clinical observation especially where excessively intense ideas [signifiers in Lacan's terms] were concerned—in hysteria and obsession, in which the quantitative characteristic emerges more plainly than in the normal [processes]. Processes such as stimulus, substitution, conversion and discharge, which had to be described there (in connection with those disorders) directly suggested the conception of neuronal excitation as quantity in a state of flow. [...] Starting from this consideration, it was possible to lay down a basic principle

of neuronal activity in relation to Q (quantity of energy). [...] This is the principle of neuronal *inertia*: neurones tend to divest themselves of Q. [...] Reflex movement is now intelligible as an established form of this giving-off: the principle provides the motive for reflex movement. [...] A primary nervous system makes use of this $Q\eta$ which it has thus acquired, by giving it off through a connecting path to the muscular mechanisms, and in that way keeps itself free from stimulus. This discharge represents the primary function of the nervous system. Here is room for the development of a secondary function.

The principle of *inertia* is, however, broken through from the first owing to another circumstance. [...] the nervous system receives stimuli from the somatic element itself—endogenous stimuli—which also have to be discharged. These have their origin in the cells of the body and give rise to the major needs: hunger, respiration, sexuality. [These "endogenous stimuli" are the precursors of the drives]. From these the organism cannot withdraw as it does from external stimuli; it cannot employ their Q for flight from the stimulus. They only cease in particular conditions, which must be realised in the external world. In order to accomplish such a *specific* action an effort is required which is independent of endogenous $Q\eta$ and in general greater, since the individual is being subjected to conditions which may be described as the *exigencies of life*. In consequence, the nervous system is obliged to abandon its original trend to inertia (that is, to bringing the level $Q\eta$ to zero). It must put up with [maintaining] a store of $Q\eta$ sufficient to meet the demand for a specific action. Nevertheless, the manner in which it does this shows that the same trend persists, modified into an endeavour at least to keep the $Q\eta$ as low as possible and to guard against any increase of it—that is, to keep it constant. [This is what was later known as the "principle of constancy" attributed by Freud to Fechner, and further on called homeostasis]. All the functions of the nervous system can be comprised either under the aspect of the primary function or of the secondary one imposed by the exigencies of life. (1895, pp. 295–297)

The subject emerges with the development of this secondary function, which is dependent on the condition of never attaining total satisfaction and remaining open to the demands of the drives.

References

Bouvet, M. (1956). La clinique psychanalytique: la relation d'objet. In: S. Nacht (Ed.), *La Psychanalyse d'aujourd'hui*: 41–121. Paris: Presses Universitaire de France.

Darriba, V. (2005). A falta conceituada por Lacan: da Coisa ao objeto *a*. *Ágora*, 8: 63–76.

Freud, S. (1895). Project for a scientific psychology. *S. E.*, 1: 281–392. London: Hogarth, 1966.

Freud, S. (1905d). Three essays on the theory of sexuality. *S. E.*, 7: 123–243. London: Hogarth, 1953.

Freud, S. (1915c). Instincts and their vicissitudes. *S. E.*, 14: 109–140. London: Hogarth, 1957.

Freud, S. (1920g). Beyond the pleasure principle. *S. E.*, 18: 1–64. London: Hogarth, 1955.

Freud, S. (1923e). The infantile genital organization. *S. E.*, 19: 139–145. London: Hogarth, 1961.

Kaplan, R. (1999). *The Nothing That Is. A Natural History of Zero*. London: Oxford University Press.

Lacan, J. (1956–1957). *Le Séminaire, Livre IV, La relation d'objet*. J. -A. Miller (Ed.). Paris: Seuil, 1994.

Lacan, J. (1959–1960). *The Seminar of Jacques Lacan, Book VII, The Ethics of Psychoanalysis*. J. -A. Miller (Ed.), D. Porter (Trans.). New York: Norton, 1992.

Lacan, J. (1960–1961). *Le Séminaire, Livre VIII, Le transfer*. J. -A. Miller (Ed.). Paris: Seuil, 1991.

Lacan, J. (1963–1964). *The Seminar of Jacques Lacan, Book XI, The Four Fundamental Concepts of Psychoanalysis*. J. -A. Miller (Ed.), A. Sheridan (Trans.). London: Penguin, 1994.

Lacan, J. (1969–1970). *The Seminar of Jacques Lacan, Book XVII, The Other Side of Psychoanalysis*. J. -A. Miller (Ed.), R. Grigg (Trans.). New York: Norton, 2007.

Lacan, J. (1970). Radiophonie. *Scilicet*, 2/3: 55–99.

Lacan, J. (1972–1973). *The Seminar of Jacques Lacan, Book XX, Encore*. J. -A. Miller (Ed.), B. Fink (Trans.). New York: Norton, 1999.

Razavet, J. -C. (2000). *De Freud a Lacan. Du roc de la castration au roc de la structure*. Paris: De Boeck and Larcier.

Shakespeare, W. (1959). King Lear. In: W. J. Craig (Ed.), *The Complete Works of William Shakespeare*: 908–942. London: Oxford University Press.

Wine, N. (1992). *Pulsão e inconsciente. A sublimação e o advento do sujeito*. (*The Drive and the unconscious. Sublimation and the advent of the subject.*). Rio de Janeiro: Jorge Zahar.

CHAPTER FOUR

Hysteria and obsession

Astrid Gessert

Freud's first formulations

Hysteria is closely connected with the very start of the development of psychoanalysis. Freud had become intrigued by this form of human suffering when, early in his career, he had become something like a confidant to his older colleague Breuer, who disclosed to him details of his innovative work with his patient Bertha Pappenheim, who would become famous in psychoanalytic literature as Anna O (Freud, 1895d, pp. 21–47). The young woman suffered from numerous medically inexplicable physical symptoms, and Breuer's treatment consisted in encouraging her to speak in a trance-like state, to tell her story, which brought temporarily relief. When, a few years later, Freud had the opportunity to observe Charcot's demonstrations of treating hysterical patients with hypnotic suggestion, his interest in this form of neurotic disturbance was revived and spurred him on in his endeavour to develop the theory of the psychical mechanisms and treatment of neurosis that became psychoanalysis.

In the paper "On the psychical mechanism of hysterical phenomena: Preliminary communication" (Freud, 1893a),[1] Freud, in collaboration with Breuer, outlined their first understanding of neurosis.

They explained the development of hysterical symptoms—such as muscular pains, paralyses, vomiting—for which no somatic causes could be found in terms of trapped affects. Affects that had been naturally aroused had become blocked at a moment of trauma, when the patient had been unable to react to the situation and release the affects it evoked. The "cathartic" cure, that Breuer had first used with Bertha P, consisted in hypnotising the patient and leading her back to the event that was connected with the symptoms, but not remembered in a wakeful state.[2] The patient would then experience the original psychical processes involved in this situation again, including the accompanying affects, which could now be released. The cure was thought to be achieved through a discharge of trapped affects. The emphasis on abreaction of affect distinguishes this early "psychotherapeutic" method, as Freud called it in his chapter on "The psychotherapy of hysteria" (Freud, 1895d, pp. 253–305), from the psychoanalytic form of work that Freud soon began to develop.

Already in their early work Breuer and Freud had made some remarkable discoveries. They had noticed that symptoms never have an independent existence, since the trauma is always in some form present within them. This led them to their well-known statement that "hysterics suffer mainly from reminiscences" and not just from symptoms (Freud, 1893a, p. 7). The symptom is a memory symbol of a forgotten trauma. They had also shown how affects are not only discharged through acts or physiological processes; human beings can use language as a surrogate for the act of abreaction. Speaking can become the adequate act of release, for example, when articulating a painful secret. In fact, the normal, non-hysterical way of dealing with psychic trauma always involves language, as the memory of the trauma is made part of a wider network of associations; via these links with other ideas, its impact becomes diminished. This is what has not happened in hysteria. The traumatic memory has not been integrated into the normal conscious complex of associations, it cannot be found in the conscious memory of the patient; she cannot speak about it. The traumatic idea is cut off from conscious ideas but remains linked to other unconscious material. Already here we find the idea of an organisation, a structure of the unconscious, which Freud would elaborate later in his article "Repression" (Freud, 1915d).

The hypnotic treatment that Freud used at this time to help patients retrieve their lost memories did not always result in the desired effect of relieving their symptoms. Consequently, Freud began to examine more thoroughly the aetiology of the neuroses he encountered, and he eventually abandoned the use of hypnosis, replacing it with the demand that patients should freely articulate all the thoughts that came into their minds. His explorations led him to distinguish two basic groups of neuroses: the "actual neuroses", which are caused by somatic factors without the involvement of psychic processes, resulting from the accumulation of tension in the body that cannot be adequately discharged, and the "psycho-neuroses", whose origin is psychological, involving an attempt by the psyche to deal with a traumatic experience. Within this latter group Freud distinguished hysteria, obsession, phobia, and hallucinatory psychosis (see Freud, 1894a; 1895d, Chapter IV: "The psychotherapy of hysteria"; 1896b; 1898a).

The basic process that he thought is involved in all cases of neurotic development begins with a conflict and ends in a symptom. An event or a thought that is incompatible with already existing ideas has entered a person's mental life. The content of the problematic idea is primarily sexual and produces troubling affects. Instead of thinking through the contradictions this idea poses, and working out some solution, a defence is set up which amounts to attempts of shutting out the idea and forgetting about it. When such attempts are only partially successful, the symptom appears as a reminder, as a memory symbol. It represents the problematic idea and the affect attached to it.

In the attempt to, if not eliminate, at least weaken the incompatible idea, the affect belonging to it becomes severed from the idea. What remains is an idea without affect and an affect without an idea. This, Freud thought, happens in all neurotic structures. But from this point on idea and affect can have different fates: in hysteria, the energy of the affect is converted into a somatic symptom, the repressed returns in the body; in obsession and phobia[3] the affect remains in the domain of the psyche, where it becomes attached to another, more acceptable idea that is compatible with the nature of the affect. This newly charged idea can then, due to its wrong connection with the persisting affect, develop into an obsessional idea, while the original idea remains conscious, but appears as unimportant. Here, the repressed returns in the mind. The form the hysterical symptom takes and the content of the obsessional idea are not arbitrary, but are in some intricate way linked with the original trauma: they are substitutes for the incompatible idea. Psychoanalytic work, making use of the patient's network of associations, can then proceed along these pathways to uncover the problematic idea.

This basic model of the development of the neuroses was elaborated further as Freud developed his theory, especially when, having abandoned hypnosis and realising that his patients could resist by refusing to speak about certain things, he recognised the importance of repression (Freud, 1915d). But Freud's main idea that neurosis starts with a conflict and ends in a symptom, with defence as the essential intervening mechanism, remained the same. It was in line with the tradition of dynamic psychology that informed Freud's education before he embarked on developing his interest in the neuroses. Influenced by both Herbartian psychology and Helmholtzian physics, he gave a central place to the interplay of forces in the organism, and in particular to the opposing tendencies of attraction and repulsion. This dualism appears in every stage of Freud's theory, until his final works. Asked to contribute an article on psychoanalysis to the *Encyclopaedia Britannica* he wrote that from a dynamic standpoint, "psychoanalysis derives all mental processes [...] from the interplay of forces, which assist or inhibit one another, combine with one another, enter into compromises with one another, etc." (Freud, 1926f, p. 265).

Hysteria and obsession in Lacanian theory

While Freud emphasised the dynamic aspect in his theory of the neuroses, Lacan approached the question of neurotic development from a structural point of view, which also informed his distinction between the fundamental clinical structures of neurosis, psychosis, and perversion. Central to Lacan's understanding is the idea that, as speaking beings, we are faced with an enigma, the enigma of our being. There is, so to speak, a black hole at the centre of our being, an incomprehensible void that is constitutive of our being. We can only "be" because there is a void, a lack-of-being ("manque a être"). This lack corresponds to a fundamental loss.

In Freud's work the idea of loss is less privileged, however, he had conceptualised loss in a number of ways. Early in his work, in his "Project for a scientific psychology" (Freud, 1895), Freud had argued that development starts with the loss of a primary experience of satisfaction and of homeostasis. The imbalance that the infant experiences leads to attempts to regain the original equilibrium, and to achieve this the organism begins to engage with the world. Later Freud used the myth of the murder of the primal father to conceptualise the fundamental loss (Freud, 1912–1913, pp. 141–155). The primal father represents the single human being who can satisfy himself completely, as he has all the women. But complete satisfaction means paralysis, stagnation, lack of desire. For things to move, the father had to be killed. The killing of the primal father stands for the origin of the symbolic dimension of human experience and society. The symbol itself relates to a killing, the symbol is the murder of the Thing, it takes the place of the Thing, but it is not the same as the Thing. The fundamental loss to which this killing by symbols leads, the gap it opens up and the enigma it creates, can itself not be symbolised. It is part of the register that Lacan called the real. But the symbolic register that comes into force with the killing of the Thing has an impact on that real that it circumscribes. It is the intersection of the symbolic and the real that configures psychical structure, the subjects relation to the object, the Other and desire.[4]

Psychical structure relates to how the speaking being deals with the fundamental loss it has suffered on entering the symbolic world and being subjected to symbolic castration. The specific way the subject manages his loss corresponds to the specific clinical structures of neurosis, psychosis, and perversion. There is no structure for normality because every subject is traumatised by the fundamental loss and faced with the impossibility of retrieving what is absent. The gap cannot be filled again, it can only be managed in various ways. The neurotic subject manages it through repression, by excluding the knowledge of his lack from consciousness; the psychotic subject deals with it more radically through foreclosing any knowledge of his lack; and the perverse subject disavows the lack by putting something—the fetish—in its place.

This understanding of the differences between the main clinical structures differs fundamentally from diagnoses that are based on the symptoms patients present, a practice that prevails in psychiatry. Taking his bearings from Freud, though developing the latter's ideas along new conceptual pathways, Lacan proposed that neurosis, psychosis, and perversion are specific ways in which the subject positions himself in relation to loss; within the realm of neurosis the structures of hysteria and obsession both relate to the particular ways repression, as a form of symbolic substitution, works in dealing with this loss.

The question of loss[5]

As loss is central to the concept of clinical structure in general, and of hysteria and obsession in particular, it is important to understand more specifically what this loss involves. While Freud had thought about the loss of homeostasis and satisfaction, Lacan spoke of the loss of the object of desire. The loss of the object is related to the separation of the child from the mother as Other. Lacan thought of this process as a logical moment, rather than as a chronological sequence. This is worth emphasising, as the terms used to describe this process are usually connected with chronological progression.

At the initial stage of the coming into being of the subject, of a speaking being as distinct from the living being, there is not yet a subject (S), an object (*a*) and an Other (A) (A stands for French: Autre = Other); the breast, for instance, forms part of the baby itself, who finds himself stuck onto the mother (see Figure 1). It comes as a moment of surprise to the baby when he notices that he can hold onto and let go of the breast, that the breast is a separable fragment. At this moment, the breast becomes a "cedable" object, an object that can become detached from the child. As the child comes into his own being as a subject, he loses not the mother, but this object, which is not the actual breast but what the breast incarnates, something that had brought the child immense pleasure. From then on this object functions as cause of desire, referred to by Lacan as object *a* (see Figure 2).[6]

The specific ways in which the subject positions himself in relation to the object of desire in his phantasy, to the Other from which he has

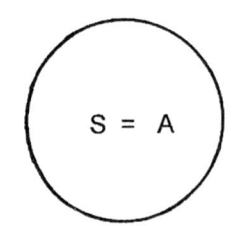

Figure 1.

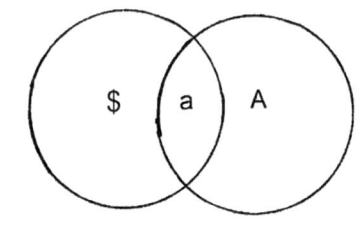

Figure 2.

separated, and to the desire that arises from this loss, constitute clinical structure. We can now turn to the specific positions of hysteria and obsession.

The obsessional structure

The obsessional deals with the loss of the object and with the corresponding separation by positioning himself in his phantasy in such a way that he can restore wholeness and unity through addition of the object. In his phantasy, he assumes that he has the object and refuses to acknowledge that he lacks something.

This can take various concrete forms which clinicians will be familiar with: for example, the patient who is predominantly interested in accumulating money, so that he never risks to "be without", to lack anything or to depend on anybody; or the person who is involved with several partners at the same time, so that somebody is always at hand; or people who swamp their friends and colleagues with their inexhaustible wealth of encyclopaedic knowledge, forestalling all questions since they have all the answers; or the patient who offers his analyst a higher fee than has been asked for in an attempt to prevent the Other from asking for something and thereby exposing lack and desire.

It is not only his own lack that the obsessional tries to evade but also the lack in the Other. This impacts on his relation to the Other. By assuming that he has the object, the obsessional also refuses to recognise and acknowledge that the object is related to an Other. Treating the object as part of himself, as his possession, he can negate the Other's existence and, most importantly, the Other's desire, which would point to a lack. In his phantasy, the obsessional is the unbarred, undivided subject who has the object, while the Other does not exist (see Figure 3).

This phantasy shapes the relationships of the obsessional in all fields of life, including professional, erotic and analytic settings. In the analytic space, obsessional analysands may treat their analysts like vending machines whom they pay, expect to function, and to produce what they have been paid for, and who can be exchanged for other analysts if they don't fulfil what is supposed to be their part of the contract. In erotic relationships, the obsessional is prone to avoid acknowledging that the object he needs to complete himself has anything to do with his actual partner. As Lacan remarked in *Seminar XX*: man "never deals with anything by way of a partner but object *a* […]. He is unable

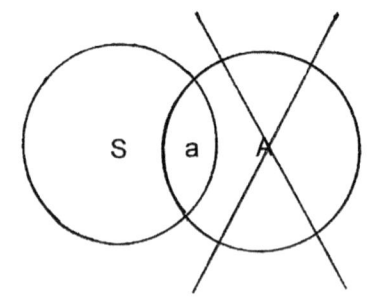

Figure 3.

to attain his sexual partner, who is the Other, except inasmuch as his partner is the cause of his desire." (1972–1973, p. 80). The partner is not seen as a desiring Other, but as the object of desire.

Annihilating the partner as Other often involves manoeuvres by which the obsessional makes sure that he does not become a cause of sexual excitement for the Other, as this could lead to an encounter with the Other's desire. This, in turn, would evoke the anxiety of being eclipsed by the Other. Concrete manifestations of such manoeuvres are the familiar scenarios staged by men who create two classes of women in their phantasy: the mother figure or saint who is the object of their filial devotion and may be represented by their actual partner, and the whore who excites and arouses them. Whores are interchangeable, they do not desire and they give what they are paid for; they do not embody a partner, but an exciting object. Avoiding intimate relationships altogether and finding satisfaction through autoerotic, masturbatory activities which allow a phantasmatic relationship with the object to be maintained without being dependent on any Other are also common variations of this theme.

By creating such closed systems the obsessional can remain quite self-sufficient. As long as he is able to maintain his system, there is no need for him to turn to an Other—to an analyst, for example—to manage his lack. Problems occur when the obsessional has an unexpected encounter with the Other, or, more precisely, with the Other's desire and *jouissance*. This had happened to Freud's "Rat Man" patient when he witnessed the terrifying *jouissance* of the cruel captain (Freud, 1909d). When the obsessional can no longer neutralise the Other, his closed system breaks down and opens up to something that causes anxiety: the real object that is related to *jouissance*, and the ultimate lack that had been covered by the phantasy object the obsessional has been holding on to. The anxiety this encounter evokes is what might induce an obsessional subject to seek help by turning to an analyst.

The hysterical structure

In cases of hysteria, the situation is different. The hysterical subject attempts to manage her lack not by producing a phantasy that places her in relation to the object that has been lost but by imagining herself as the object that the Other is missing (see Figure 4).

She engages with her own lack by way of the Other's lack and she tries to constitute herself as the object that would complete the Other, that would plug the Other's desire. We have seen that the obsessional strives to complete himself as subject; the hysteric, on the other hand, does not constitute herself as subject but as object for the Other. Rather than being a desiring subject and looking for an object to meet her desire, "the hysteric seeks to divine the Other's desire and to become the particular object that, when missing, makes the Other desire" (Fink, 1997, p. 120). In this way, she defines her being.

What is of importance in the manoeuvres of the hysteric is her engagement with the desire of the Other. She is not interested in satisfying this desire but in keeping the Other's desire alive, "since as long as the Other desires, her position as object is assured: a space is guaranteed for her within the Other" (ibid., p. 120). Therefore she attempts to sustain the Other's desire not simply by offering herself as a tantalising object, but by offering herself as an object that keeps slipping away,

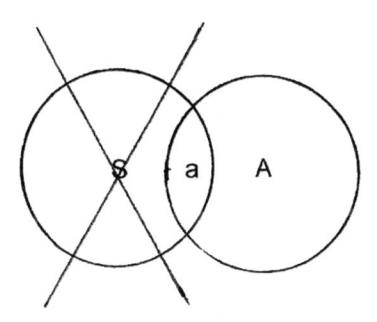

Figure 4.

thus ensuring a lack of satisfaction and a continuation of desire (Lacan, *Écrits*, 1966, p. 698; Soler, 1996, p. 269).

Common examples of such manoeuvres are the involvement in triangular situations where a woman becomes fascinated by "the other woman", attempts to identify desirable features in this woman, and tries to direct her partner's attention to these, imagining that her partner desires what the other woman has. At the same time, the hysteric may also identify with her supposedly desiring partner, thus making his desire hers. If the partner is not demonstrative in expressing his desire, if he proves to be too predictable and reliable, the woman may complain about being bored.

At the centre of the hysteric's manoeuvres is always an unsatisfied desire. She avoids satisfying her partner and she deprives herself. In erotic encounters, she may fantasise that another woman is in bed with her partner, or that her partner is somebody else, thus avoiding being the cause of his enjoyment since either she or he is not present (Soler, 1996, p. 269; Fink, 1997, p. 127). In the analytic setting, such patients may try to provoke the analyst's desire by presenting themselves as enigmas. They may turn up late or not at all, to keep the Other puzzled and in suspense, or they respond to a poignant interpretation or intervention by producing a new symptom to evoke new questions. While the obsessional tries to neutralise and eclipse the Other, the hysteric emphasises the importance of the Other, she needs the Other to define her own being. By fantasising what would complete the Other, and then orchestrating scenarios so that the Other's desire remains unsatisfied, she hopes to secure a permanent position as desired object.

Both, the obsessional and the hysteric subject refuse to be the cause of the Other's enjoyment for fear of disappearing as subject, but they do so in different ways. The obsessional's refusal reflects his attempt to annul the Other and his desire, while the hysteric's refusal is an attempt to keep the desire of the Other alive. What is at stake for both of them is their position as subject, to which the Other poses a threat. A sexual encounter between an obsessional and a hysteric subject could thus take the form of him talking and thinking of anything but the woman he is having sex with, so that he does not lose himself and fade as subject, while she imagines that she is in bed with somebody else, thereby refusing to be the cause of his enjoyment.

Transference and treatment

The different positions that the obsessional and the hysteric occupy in relation to the object, to the Other, and to desire have implications for the transference and treatment.

The obsessional sees himself as a whole, unbarred subject who is the master of his fate, rather than as somebody subjected to lack and subject to an Other. This situation makes him an unlikely candidate for seeking analysis, as analysis means enlisting the help of an Other. The point at which the obsessional may turn to analysis is often precipitated by an unexpected encounter with the Other and the Other's desire and *jouissance*, as the Rat Man experienced in the company of the cruel captain (Freud, 1909d). Such an experience can bring his attempts to neutralise the Other, and his usual ways of managing his lack, into disarray. This will cause anxiety and can open the way to seek assistance from an Other. However, having entered the consulting room, such patients will often seek help rather than knowledge, and will soon revert to their familiar strategies of trying to obliterate the Other. As what is Other is also the unconscious, the obsessional's attempt to ignore the Other will appear in the treatment as a refusal to acknowledge the workings of the unconscious. We have seen that in obsession the repressed returns in the mind, which means that he can speak the repressed, but he does not know what he is saying, and he does not want to hear this other discourse by which we are spoken, which makes us say and do things we do not intend (Soler, 1996, p. 263). In analytic sessions, this can mean that the obsessional has difficulties in producing associations, is monosyllabic in his responses, and may claim that he has few memories. Instead, he will present facts, theories, and stringent logical arguments. Or he may speak incessantly, leaving no room for any gaps in which anything other than his premeditated discourse could irrupt. He may pay little attention to what the analyst is saying, talk over him, and deliver his own interpretations, rejecting any ideas that do not fit into his system of thought, thus demonstrating his mastery and independence. He will not address the analyst as "subject-supposed-to-know", as placeholder of "what the unconscious knows about the subject" (ibid., p. 276; see also Lacan, *Seminar XI*, 1963–1964, Chapter Eighteen).

This scenario requires the analyst not to affirm the obsessional's phantasy in which the Other is annihilated. He must pay particular attention to any moment when the patient shows signs of being a bit more attentive to the Other and to what the Other wants, and bring his own desire to know into play, insisting that there is more to know than what is obvious.

The hysteric is in a different position. As she depends on the Other and the Other's desire to manage her lack-of-being, she finds it easy to turn to an Other for help. She may start an analysis with the idea that the analyst will tell her who she is, what her symptoms mean, what she should do to become a happier person, etc. However, if the analyst attempts to supply the knowledge she requests, she tends to invalidate it, by questioning, evaluating, and rejecting it. Seeking the lack in the Other, she seeks the lack in the analyst's knowledge, so that she can supplement it and, at the same time, produce another question for him. She re-enacts her wish to remain an enigma for the Other, the enigmatic object that causes desire.

The shift that has to occur in the transference is that rather than making the analyst work for her and asking him about his desire, the hysteric has to start working for herself; instead of asking her analyst, she has to ask her unconscious "What do you want?". This is the place the analyst has to occupy: he has to become the enigma that she questions, and in relation to which she can produce her phantasy of what it is that the Other wants.

The knowledge that both the hysteric and the obsessional can produce in the analytic work can result in a fundamental shift in the subject's relation to loss by recognising that loss is constitutive of the subject and that it is neither inflicted by, nor can it be resolved by, the Other. At this point, the subject can, as Colette Soler puts it, "stop asking the Other to resolve his castration" (Soler, 1996, p. 278).

Conclusion

In Lacan's understanding the distinction between hysteria and obsession is a structural distinction in terms of how the subject, who is always lacking, situates himself in relation to the object that is lacking, to the Other who has some affinity to this object, and to desire which arises from this lack. Psychoanalysis does not aim at filling this lack and producing a subject that is complete, and neither is its goal to abolish the neurotic structures. In the analytic process, the analysand has the chance to encounter and confront his lack, rather than avoiding it, and to assume the desire that arises from it. This entails a process of separation that leads to greater freedom: for the obsessional, from the object he tries to hold on to, and for the hysteric, from the desire of the Other on which she depends.

Notes

1. This paper became the introductory chapter to *Studies on Hysteria* (1895d).
2. I will use the pronoun "she" when speaking about hysteric patients, and "he" when speaking about obsessional patients, as, thinking in terms of the structures of hysteria and obsession, it is more common to find hysteria in women, who want "it", than in men who have "it", but fear to lose it.
3. Freud thought initially that phobia is closely related to obsession. Later he suggested: "In the classificatory system of the neuroses no definite position has hitherto been assigned to 'phobias'. It seems certain that they should only be regarded as syndromes which may form part of various neuroses and that we need not rank them as an independent pathological process." He further suggests that phobias share a similar psychological structure to hysteria and most frequently take the form of anxiety hysteria (1909d, p. 115; see also 1915d).
4. "Thus the symbol manifests itself first of all as the killing of the thing, and this death results in the endless perpetuation of the subject's desire." (Lacan, 1966, p. 262)
5. In presenting the ideas in the sections on the function of loss and on the structures of obsession and hysteria I have closely followed the exposition of Fink on the subject of neurosis, from whom I have also borrowed some poignant formulations and the figures 1–3, and 4 (Fink, 1997, Chapter Eight, esp. pp. 119–121), which relate to Lacan's elaboration of the relation of the subject and the Other in *Seminar XI* (Lacan, 1963–1964, Chapters Sixteen and Seventeen, pp. 203–229). A very useful elaboration of the differential diagnosis of hysteria and obsession, on which I have also drawn, has been presented by Colette Soler (1996), who explores particularly the hysteric's and obsessional's relation to desire.
6. See Lacan, 1962–1963, *Seminar X*, session: 12th July 1963, and 1963–1964, *Seminar XI*, Chapters Sixteen and Seventeen; Fink, 1997, Chapter Eight.

References

Fink, B. (1997). *A Clinical Introduction to Lacanian Psychoanalysis*. Cambridge, MA and London: Harvard.

Freud, S. (1894a). *The neuro-psychoses of defence. S. E., 3*. London: Hogarth, 1962, 41–68.
Freud, S. (1895). *Project for a scientific psychology. S. E., 1*: 281–392. London: Hogarth, 1966.
Freud, S. (1896b). *Further remarks on the neuro-psychoses of defence. S. E., 3*: 157–185. London: Hogarth, 1962.
Freud, S. (1898a). *Sexuality in the aetiology of the neuroses. S. E., 3*: 259–285. London: Hogarth, 1962.
Freud, S. (1909d). *Notes upon a case of obsessional neurosis. S. E., 10*: 151–318. London: Hogarth, 1955.
Freud, S. (1912–1913). *Totem and taboo. S. E., 13*: vii–162. London: Hogarth, 1953.
Freud, S. (1915d). *Repression. S. E., 14*: 141–158. London: Hogarth, 1957.
Freud, S. (1926f). *Psycho-analysis. S. E., 20*: 257–270. London: Hogarth, 1959.
Freud, S., & Breuer, J. (1893a). *On the psychical mechanism of hysterical phenomena: Preliminary communication. S. E., 2*: 3–17. London: Hogarth, 1955.
Freud, S., & Breuer, J. (1895d). *Studies on Hysteria. S. E., 2*. London: Hogarth, 1955.
Lacan, J. (1962–1963). *Le Séminaire, Livre X, L'Angoisse*. J. -A. Miller (Ed.). Paris: Seuil, 2004.
Lacan, J. (1963–1964). *The Seminar of Jacques Lacan, Book XI, The Four Fundamental Concepts of Psychoanalysis*. J. -A. Miller (Ed.), A. Sheridan (Trans.). London: Penguin, 1994.
Lacan, J. (1966). *Écrits*. B. Fink (Trans.). New York and London: Norton, 2002.
Lacan, J. (1972–1973). *The Seminar of Jacques Lacan, Book XX, Encore*. J. -A. Miller (Ed.), B. Fink (Trans.). New York and London: Norton, 1999.
Soler, C. (1996). Hysteria and obsession. In: R. Feldstein, B. Fink, & M. Jaanus (Eds.), *Reading Seminars I and II* (pp. 248–282). Albany, NY: State University of New York, 1996.

CHAPTER FIVE

An introductory journey in transference

Vincent Dachy

Departure

In the late nineteen century Sigmund Freud became convinced that some symptoms were determined by unconscious motives, and he set out to demonstrate this fact. How "obvious" this may appear to us today only shows how easily cutting-edge ideas may become blunt and fall into stuporous common sense as soon as they enter what is curiously called "public knowledge". Very curious indeed, as public knowledge appears to equate to a knowledge that we have lost sight of, whereas for Freud—and for those who continue to keep his endeavour alive—it is precisely the reverse that had always been at stake: to articulate the principles of a knowledge so private that "unreasonable", "irrational", "devilish" even, have been words used to qualify it.

Whether or not other people were walking along the same kind of path with Freud at the same epoch will not preoccupy us here, as our focus lies elsewhere. We will try to delineate how, in the adventure of psychoanalysis, something called "transference" should have appeared—appeared and stayed. Even if many may believe that psychoanalysis would be a lot easier without it, all psychoanalysts have also to accept that psychoanalysis could not take place without it. It soon became a crucial notion in psychoanalysis for the simple reason that it stands at the centre of the conception(s) of the direction of the treatment. The most serious attempt at theorising transference after Freud was no doubt that of Jacques Lacan who re-centred transference on the question of knowledge, when, after Freud, a wave of "feelings" seemed to have overwhelmed many psychoanalysts. However, we will not opt for the historical view here but will rather try to elicit the main points that, we think, allow us to circumscribe the domain of transference. We will also try to show that transference is a journey and not a static affair.

It came as a surprise

As Freud was gradually testing his hypothesis of the unconscious and refining his discoveries he came up against certain phenomena he did not expect. Some patients seemed to develop certain feelings about him, feelings beyond the trust you would expect from a patient to his/her "doctor". Let us say feelings of a more passionate nature. And these seemed to be particularly linked to interpretations that Freud had made. The problem, really, was that these feelings did not accompany his interpretations as a sign of gratitude or enlightenment but rather seemed to cloud or obliterate these interpretations. Moreover, these feelings were not necessarily positive. It was not simply that patients might disagree with some of his interpretations, in the sense that a given interpretation could prove to be incorrect. In those cases indifference was to be expected, rather than passionate reactions. Even more surprising were the manifestations of affection, the interest or curiosity taken in the person of the analyst, the apparent docility shown by the patient while the analysis did not really progress. Freud's surprise was that knowledge might therefore not be the paramount prize sought by all.[1]

It came as a bad surprise

So, the attainment of unconscious knowledge would not be reached without difficulties. The patient who, supposedly, was to benefit from the effects of interpretation was the very one to oppose this beneficial knowledge. Which seemed rather dispiriting. If Freud was surprised he was not astounded. He had had occasion to notice that there was resistance against the emergence of unconscious material. After all, the idea of repression was that "something" important to the patient had been kept out of the realm of consciousness despite the possible ciphered manifestations of this unknown something. The bad surprise was not so much that the situation of the analysis was not sufficient to easily free patients from their resistances: after all, Freud had started with hypnosis as a way to enlarge the field of consciousness, only to abandon that practice, which proved to be incompatible with his determination to elaborate knowledge, and his observations that the symptomatic improvements obtained through hypnosis did not have the consequences he wished for. Freud was already aware that resistances had to be reckoned with and that the setting of the analysis was not enough in itself to dissipate them all. No, the bad surprise was that the person of the analyst got entangled with the resistance. This was clear to Freud, for whom anything that hindered the analytic process was resistance; and indeed transferential feelings did not facilitate or speed up the analysis. It all seemed rather complicated. If anyone had thought the process of an analysis would reside in the straightforward communication of perhaps uncomfortable but life-changing information, well, it was not the case.

Early in his work Freud had become familiar with the idea of displacement, the displacement of a representation by another one and the displacement of a charge of affect from one representation to another. Even a slip of the tongue, amongst other manifestations of the unconscious, could easily be conceived as a transfer from one word to another, bearing witness to the presence of an unconscious motive. But if transference involved the person of the analyst it would render the disclosure of desire more difficult, as it would have to be told to the very person concerned.

Freud, not work-shy, thought that each and every transference (i.e. every occurrence of transference) would have to be treated like any other symptom and, hopefully, be got rid of, which might have meant the resolution of transference as an obstacle to the treatment. But would Freud see the end of it all if every interpretation of transference contributed to fuel it at the same time?[2]

It came as a good surprise

Through the advances in his practice, Freud produced the theory of the Oedipus complex, which had a direct effect on the question of transference. As the Oedipus theory was in actual fact a theory of relations—that of the infant to his parents—including twists, turns, and ambivalence, it only followed logically that transference be considered within that framework. Transference got referred to the relations patients had had with their parents. Hostility, tenderness or ambivalence in transference ceased to be mysterious. But this resolution of mystery was not the good surprise. After all, it did not alter the fact that transference served the resistance. No, the good surprise was a chance, the chance of a second chance. Transference presented a second chance to the drive motives, the drive stakes, the *Triebregungen* that could not find an outlet first time round, by way of their actualisation in the transference, through their enactment in relation to the analyst. Freud called this phenomenon "transference neurosis" and it became an important part of the analysis itself. Inasmuch as it could be considered a repetition of some aspects of the relations to the parents, it was also actual and, with the interventions of the analyst, possibly the occasion for something new. So transference had now become a path of possible change.[3]

But they did not live happily ever after

Again Freud seemed to have transformed an obstacle into a lever—as he had been doing so cunningly and perceptively with whatever his practice had thrown at him. By now, it seemed that transference had become the motor of the treatment. To put it very generally, transference was the operating engine of the analysis, inasmuch as the patient, wanting the approval of the analyst, found this a good enough reason to participate in the work of the analysis.

The years following the First World War gradually led Freud to somewhat different conclusions: transference conceived as the mobilisation of certain drives whose vicissitudes had not ceased to trouble the patient—particularly in relation to his parents—appeared to have reached its limits. Up against what Freud came to call "Thanatos", or the "death drive", transference seemed to have found the limit of its power. The consequence Freud had to accept was an unsettling one. Both his practice and his observations of *"Kultur"* brought him to the conclusion that human beings were not prepared to give up their unconscious phantasy. If nothing else the "negative therapeutic reaction" was sufficient proof of this. Freud realised that some patients were attached to their symptoms, to their suffering, more than to anything else and that the analytic work was somehow becoming part of giving that suffering a prominent place rather than leading the patient to abandon such investment. This did not invalidate what Freud had elaborated until then but it somehow substantiated a limit to the powers of psychoanalysis. Did Freud accept this easily? I suppose not, as he had spent a lifetime finding breakthroughs.[4]

Suspended conclusion

So, when the invitation is made to a patient to say whatever comes to mind, without reservation, you may indeed get a transference of words and representations, but you could also get a suspension, inhibition or even an entrenched stasis of the associative process. In the place of "free associations" come thoughts and feelings related to the presence and/or the person of the analyst. And these thoughts often disrupt the tracks of associations, replacing remembering by some actual display. But for Freud the display became the occasion of a replay of what was playing up the patient, up to the point where it seemed that the analysis encountered something so vital to the patient that there was no question for him but to put it into play. The castration complex, the unconscious phantasy, the fundamental trauma were different ways of designating this limit to the analysis that transference could not overcome. At least this limit seemed to question the furthest possible point to which an analysis could be conducted; so, the effort might not have been in vain.

Intermezzo

For a long while after Freud the theory of transference suffered no crucial changes. If anything worth noticing occurred it was rather in the ways certain analysts considered it should be handled. The "active therapy" of Ferenczi, for example, was an attempt to intervene in the transference in ways that were supposed to accelerate the process or give the analyst a position that would appear less passive—at least to Ferenczi, and give "countertransference" an important place in the direction of the treatment. If the former did not prove to be a way forward, the latter became a field in which the theory of transference got confused between the classical view that the analyst's personal feelings should have no part in his directing of the treatment and one that considered feelings on the side of the analyst—at least some feelings—as a source of understanding of/for the patient. The compatibility of both perspectives was and is, as anyone can easily imagine, a rather perilous exercise in which the intuitive and experiential notion of "feeling" plays the role if not of the quadrilateral circle then of the round square.[5]

A return to rigour

In the early 1950s Jacques Lacan started a practice of teaching the basis of which were Freud's texts and the experience of psychoanalysis. Lacan's effort was to elaborate what the crucial principles of psychoanalysis were and how they were articulated to each other. This was not a series of sporadic attempts to add a bit of meaning here or there but a general theoretical endeavour, psychoanalysis at large.

For instance, some analysts chose to stress the fact that, in the analytic situation, both the analysand and the analyst are human beings with feelings. Why? Were they afraid that anybody would believe that one of the two might not be human or not have any feelings? Had some analysts forgotten that and needed to be reminded? Or was this part of an increasing bureaucratisation, obsessionalisation of analytic practice? Lacan refocused on the parameters that made the analytic situation specific to its aim. The task was, therefore, to elaborate them as such. The analytic experience is primarily an experience of speech, therefore attention should be paid to what speech and language entail: what is the relation of a speaking being to language? Who speaks, what is being said and how, to whom is what is being said addressed, and what does matter in what is being said? Lacan had the ambition to regard the function and field of speech and language in a way that would not allow psychoanalysts to say something and its contrary—at least comfortably.[6]

Starting point

Consider this: if Mr Might thinks of starting an analysis it's because he knows that it's on offer, by Mr Hum for instance. So Mr Might can presume that someone wants him. But if it happens that Mr Might chooses Mr Hum as his analyst he will then presume that Mr Hum has something he wants.

Those who tend to obscure what matters in analysis will often try to reduce this minimal situation to a "Well, they both want *something* then" but will not consider that these wants are not the same, unless, once again, you reduce all wants to something like "want of a satisfaction of some sort". At this point everyone has to chose to either be pleased with the lowest possible denominator to figure out any situation—which does not allow us to know very much—or, instead, to go further. It is a question of going far enough to delineate what matters in psychoanalysis specifically. Adding that the transaction is nailed because Mr Might wants "to feel better" and Mr Hum wants "to make him feel better", is once again too vague. It is only when Mr Might explains what he suffers from and how, and Mr Hum verifies that there is a dimension of unknown knowledge involved, that, minimally speaking, we may then speak of a possible analysis.

So there is an asymmetry at the start of any analysis; something that is wanted: some hope, let us put it simply, on the side of the analysand-to-be; being prepared to sustain the process of analysis on the side of the analyst. One will grasp without difficulty that if the analysand is barely interested in the process of his analysis (demanding quick results for his money but without interest in what will make him feel better, for instance) and if the analyst is there only for the money, there is little chance that things will go very far. This asymmetry is precisely what creates the "domain of transference" in which both analysand and analyst are situated. It is also this asymmetry that is the basis for the commitment to the analysis from both parties.

A necessary supposition

Some people seem to have difficulties in speaking openly to anyone, including an analyst. Are they uncertain whether it is possible to entrust anybody with anything or are they too sure of its impossibility? Is it a matter of ignorance or knowledge? The important point for our topic is to realise that we cannot speak without making suppositions.

What Lacan called transference is the supposition of the analysand that there is some knowledge that concerns him, of which the analyst becomes the "location"; a place that the analyst sustains. Not that the analyst knows everything—or nothing for that matter—but that the analyst is the locus for the supposition to be addressed, to be incarnated. The fact that such supposition could take the form of a conscious idea about the analyst as clever or stupid, or that it never crossed the analysand's mind in this way is not without importance, but it does not determine the supposition in itself, which is determined by the act of speech. Having said that, it may be very difficult for such a supposition to operate if the analysand regards his analyst as being stupid a bit too often. In other terms, the supposition is linked to the act of speech but is not automatically upheld. What enables such a supposition to be located in a particular analyst can be highly variable and does not necessarily depend on the academic knowledge of the analyst, his witty mind, etc. It may amount to a seemingly insignificant something attached to the analyst that is of elective importance to the analysand, perhaps a phrase of the analyst, perhaps even something the analysand noticed when he "googled" the analyst before a first appointment or a detail in the waiting room. These examples aim at stressing the fact that the place of transference should not be confused with what/who happens to occupy it. But, still, the place has to be occupied, in the flesh.

Transference is the space that would enable the analysand to put into play what has been significant in his life, most importantly the signifiers (and their enjoyment-value) at stake in the constitution of his symptom.[7]

The woods ... and some trees hiding them

This is the way Lacan grounded transference both in the practice and in a theory of relations based on speech and language. This is "the woods" and it is time now to pay attention to the few trees that often obscure them. First of all, is everything being said by the analysand about the analyst? The difference between place and person should have taken care of this tedious question. Everything said in analysis is not about the analyst but about the analysis and is addressed to the analyst. Therefore it matters greatly that the analyst is attentive to the ways he has been addressed and to what/whose place he has been situated in. Now, of course, certain things are said about the analyst and these have to be considered in the context delineated above. This is of particular importance for the analyst's interventions because, as Lacan noticed, he will only be heard from the position he has been put in.[8]

But what about feelings then? Here again we will have to be more refined. We will choose the difference between "passions for being" as Lacan called them[8] and "affects" of which Lacan refused to establish a register, but to which he devoted an entire year of seminars, choosing the most radical one, anxiety, to make his point.[9]

A passion, an affect, can come up in an analysis without being related to the person of the analyst, even though it is addressed to the analyst. The free associations and the remembering that often comes with them may indeed bring back all kinds of impressions in the analysand. But they can also more or less suddenly, more or less transiently, and with many possible variations over time relate to the person of the analyst.

Affects are rather concerned with lack-of-being or want-to-be (desire). They accompany the occurrences of the dimension of desire and its vicissitudes. Anxiety, as the affect associated with the imminence of (the Other's) enjoyment (consumption or disappearance of the Other's desire; "the lack of the lack") shows this most radically.

Passions for being: love, hate, and—often forgotten but most important—ignorance. These feelings concern the subject inasmuch as he hopes to locate his being in the Other (*love*), as he cannot accept his (way of) being to be disputed (*hate*), as he makes sure he knows nothing about the incompleteness/inconsistency/undecidability/inexistence of the Other (*ignorance*).

Of course, in the analysand's life all these feelings may be felt and expressed, together or not. Everybody will understand that if hatred is too constantly present in an analysis it is likely that the analysand will simply interrupt the analysis. So, what is called "negative transference" is therefore the occurrence of hatred within a sufficiently workable space of transference. The occurrence of hate focused on the analyst does not necessarily annul the space of transference. If it is carefully considered it can also be a fruitful occasion. After all, it would be surprising if no feeling, ranging from disappointment to hatred, would occur in an experience that invites the analysand to say whatever crosses his mind.

And love?

We will now focus on transference love.[10] If entrusting an analyst is crucial to the opening of the space of transference and the establishment of the subject-supposed-to-know, the coming to the fore of the person of the analyst (as in: "Suddenly I realised that I know nothing about you." Or: "Well, … you must have feelings too …") should not cloud the fact that it is the passion for ignorance that is always being served. Transference love is an effect of the analytic process when, in the course of his associations, and probably in the vicinity of some troublesome thoughts, the analysand attempts to ensure that he is likeable (worthy, esteemed). It is a resort to the agency of the ideal, the ego-ideal, admiration, idealisations, etc. which has the effect of stopping the analysand in his associative path. An erotic turn of the transference can also happen whereby, again, seduction may put desire to the service of love, and ignorance. Erotic fantasies involving the analyst but not hindering the analytic process may remind us of what matters: the analysis of whatever comes to mind.

And trust?

Quite rightly it seems that what is called trust is the feeling that accompanies the opening of the field of transference. It may be less the hope of finding (an answer to) being in the Other, than the confidence, the conviction, the faith that nothing said during the process of analysis will be used by the analyst for his personal satisfaction; that the analysand will not be the object of enjoyment [*jouissance*] of the analyst. The analyst should stay clear of enjoyment (except the enjoyment of deciphering) as Lacan asserted.[11] Analysts know and accept this as a condition for psychoanalysis. Hopefully, by now, the question of transference has been clarified enough for it not to remain hazy in the cloudy concept of feeling.

No interminable love then?

In psychoanalysis love is necessary until contingency is reached. The supposition of knowledge is crucial until the knowledge does not have to be supposed any more. When knowledge attains contingency, the contingency of the analysand's singular arrangement of/with enjoyment (the real of being, we could say; the "special something" that the analysand hoped to find in the analyst; the very special something that also proved to be at the root of the analysand's phantasy), transference love is not necessary any more. It is not liquidated, it is not resolved, it is just not necessary anymore.

- Does it disappear?
- It is not necessary anymore.
- Yes, but does it disappear?
- Well, what happens when love is not necessary anymore?
- It disappears, I am sure, that is sad.
- And why should it disappear? Why should the disappearance of necessity imply the disappearance of something called love!?

Outcome

The ways a subject loves (hates and ignores) can "per-haps" (by way of the "happenings" of an analysis) change. An analysis can allow an analysand not only to unravel the determinants of his relation to being spoken and speaking, it can also happen to extract what (dis) satisfaction, what enjoyments, what encounters with enjoyment were at the core of his symptomatic arrangement—including the enjoyment involved in his demand for love.[12] One may not demand in the same way after an analysis.

This may indeed open new possibilities of loving; unnecessary ways to love, to want, and to compose, in the musical sense, the relentlessness of enjoyment. One may not love in quite the same way after an analysis.[13]

By way of conclusion: an orientated journey

We have found it useful to articulate transference according to four logical moments of the trajectory of an analysis. The following sequence indicates a possibility of thinking about transference as a space of transformations orientated by the passage from necessity to contingency. The trajectory starts with the *imposition* of signifiers onto the living being, and it enters the field of psychoanalytic practice through the *supposition* of knowledge. The analytic process, directed with humility, could lead to the *deposition* (Lacan talked about *désêtre*, disbeing) of the supposition in question, thereby extracting the singular stake that had sustained the supposition. And the analysis finds its denouement when the deposition becomes the basis of a *composition*, of a "knowing-some-how" with the trajectory itself. So, a journey: from an imposed unknown knowledge to a supposed one, and towards a deposited knowledge to the composition of a knowing-some-how.

Some remarks for further thoughts:

- Freud elaborated the primal identification as a love for the father preceding any object investment when the other identifications are defined the other way round. What are the consequences of such a statement for transference?
- For Freud, transference in psychosis was considered impossible on the basis that, in psychosis, there was no possibility of investment in anything/anybody outside the ego itself. The clinic has proved

such a radical position erroneous. Rather it seems that working with psychotic subjects calls for a more general theory of transference where it is the relation between trust and (the Other's) enjoyment that is the horizon of possible transformation.

- In *Seminar XI* Lacan stated that—this is a fundamental statement—"transference is the enactment of the reality of the unconscious", which is nothing but sexuality.[14] That begs the question of situating sexuality properly in psychoanalysis and then to articulate the enactment in question (see footnote 5). What was said above about the difference between the dimension of desire and that of love gives one a direction here.
- After *Seminar XI*, Lacan's further elaborations regarding the question of transference will focus around the question of the "desire of the psychoanalyst", the question of interpretation and particularly his stress on the "act of the psychoanalyst". This emphasises the *act* rather than the *passion*.
- It follows from the developments above that the outcome of transference is of particular interest in the case of someone who has the project to practise as an analyst.

Notes

1. The role played by hypnosis in the early stages of the invention of the psychoanalytic treatment and the reasons that made Freud decide to abandon the suggestive techniques are both relevant in the birth of the question of transference. Freud's texts of the late 1880s and early 1890s show this development.
2. This is where the involvement of the psychoanalyst (with)in the treatment becomes clearer. The psychoanalyst is not an observer but "part and parcel" of the treatment (see Freud's "Psycho-analytic procedure" (Freud, 1904a) and "On psychotherapy" (Freud, 1905a)).
3. See the major contributions between 1910 and 1915, especially perhaps "The dynamics of transference" (Freud, 1912b) and "Observations on transference-love" (Freud, 1915a).
4. Even if this apparent limit of the power of psychoanalysis might have come as a disappointment to Freud, we consider that this question has been the domain where psychoanalysis has decided and decides on its future. This limit shows that psychoanalysis does not follow the traditional (naive?) assumption of a medical treatment:

symptom > diagnosis > treatment > cure. Nor is psychoanalysis a technique that you can apply to or, worse, impose on someone. It is a possibility; it may have no contra-indication as such but it has conditions. And its outcome is not predictable from the start even if its aim can be delineated.
5. Paula Heimann's article "On counter-transference" (1950) seems to have been important in this debate.

    It should be obvious to everyone that the notion of feeling demands an explicit articulation of the question of truth (and of that of "real"). Invoking intuition at this point should not satisfy anyone concerned about the future of psychoanalysis.

    From a somewhat parallel viewpoint a critique of the notion of "need" would be most adequate and useful here to reinstate the horizon of sexuality ("enjoyment [*jouissance*] and desiring") that seems to have faded from some orientations of psychoanalysis at the same time perhaps as countertransference gathered momentum!
6. See Lacan, "The function and field of speech and language in psychoanalysis" [1953]. In: *Écrits* (1966), pp. 237–268.
7. See Lacan (1995), "Proposition of the 9th October 1967 on the Psychoanalyst of the School".
8. See Lacan, "The direction of the treatment and the principles of its power" [1958]. In: *Écrits* (1966), pp. 215–270.
9. See Lacan (1962–1963), *Seminar X: Anxiety*.
10. Can all loves be reduced to one? Love from a mother or a father, for children, for pets, for parents, for success, for broad shoulders or twinkling eyes, for the "needy", for roses …?
11. See Lacan (1973), *Television*; the end of the third part.
12. Love supports the existence of the Other and harbours the enjoyment of being as inscribed in the Other.
13. See Lacan (1972–1973), *Seminar XX: Encore*.
14. See Lacan (1963–1964), *Seminar XI: The Four Fundamental Concepts of Psychoanalysis*, p. 149.

References

Freud, S. (1904a). *Freud's psycho-analytic procedure*. S. E., 7: 247–254. London: Hogarth, 1953.

Freud, S. (1905a). *On psychotherapy*. S. E., 7: 255–268. London: Hogarth, 1953.

Freud, S. (1912b). *The dynamics of transference*. S. E., 12: 97–108. London: Hogarth, 1958.

Freud, S. (1915a). *Observations on transference love (further recommendations on the technique of psycho-analysis III)*. S. E., 12: 157–171. London: Hogarth, 1958.

Heimann, P. (1950). On counter-transference. *International Journal of Psychoanalysis, 31*: 81–84.

Lacan, J. (1962–1963). *The Seminar of Jacques Lacan, Book X, Anxiety.* J. -A. Miller (Ed.), A. Price (Trans.). Cambridge: Polity, 2014.

Lacan, J. (1963–1964). *The Seminar of Jacques Lacan, Book XI, The Four Fundamental Concepts of Psychoanalysis.* J. -A. Miller (Ed.), A. Sheridan (Trans.). London: Penguin, 1994.

Lacan, J. (1966). *Écrits. A Selection.* B. Fink (Trans.). New York: Norton, 2002.

Lacan, J. (1972–1973). *The Seminar of Jacques Lacan, Book XX, Encore.* J. -A. Miller (Ed.), B. Fink (Trans.). New York: Norton, 1999.

Lacan, J. (1973). *Television: A Challenge to the Psychoanalytic Establishment.* D. Hollier, R. Krauss, & A. Michelson (Trans.). New York: Norton, 1990.

Lacan, J. (1995). Proposition of the 9th October 1967 on the psychoanalyst of the school. R. Grigg (Trans.). *Analysis, 6*: 1–13.

CHAPTER SIX

Interpretation

Darian Leader

Psychoanalysis is certainly not the only procedure today that claims to operate on the unconscious. Most forms of therapy recognise that unconscious thought exerts an effect on our lives, yet when pressed to articulate how this part of our psyche should best be accessed, the responses are disappointing. Most of them formulate their approach in terms of learning: as children, we become stuck in unhelpful patterns of thought and behaviour, which may, indeed, succumb to repression. In therapy, it follows, they have to be "unlearnt".

Sometimes the examples of these patterns are not unconvincing, yet what has really changed in the landscape of the therapies here is the neglect of interpretation itself. If you figure out what the patient is repeating from childhood, what they might have repressed or the feelings they are denying, these should then be communicated to them. Tactfully yes, carefully yes, but communicated all the same. While there is some debate about the question of tact and care, the basic notion of communication is more or less taken for granted. Interpretation then becomes a form of learning—or unlearning followed by learning—and, as a consequence, therapy becomes an educational process.

The psychoanalytic tradition has been divided on this issue. For some analysts working today in the framework of the IPA, there is little to be discussed. Neurosis is seen as the result of a developmental disorder which analysis can correct. The contours of such disorders are known in advance, and analysis is akin to a pedagogy. The main difference with other therapeutic approaches is that the relationship between analysand and analyst is recognised to be the key variable in allowing the education to work. Interpreting the transference, then, is what allows change.

For those analysts working in the Lacanian tradition, things are rather different. Interpretation is one of the most central concepts of psychoanalysis, and requires a careful theorisation of its aims, methods and impasses. These problems were once the subject of lively debate in the IPA, yet, from the late 50s onwards, questions of interpretation became reframed as questions of ego structure, for reasons that I have tried to describe elsewhere (Leader, 1996). It was really only Lacan and his students who kept this debate open from that moment onwards.

Despite this waning of interest, it is a fact that whether they are focusing on the question of interpretation or not, analysts interpret in very different ways. Some are rather silent, while others keep up a running commentary on what they think is going on. Karl Abraham, for example, was well-known for being taciturn, while Hans Sachs was always yapping. Freud himself was fond of amusing stories and irony, while Herbert Rosenfeld believed that humour should be altogether absent from the analyst's speech.

These questions of personal style cannot be dissociated from the question of what interpretation aims at. Does it hope to educate the ego, deflate an ideal, unveil a desire, weaken an attachment or clarify a connection? Presumably different aims will be germane to different moments of an analysis, and styles will vary both between treatments and within the same treatment. One might wonder how a uniform style of interpreting could be effective throughout an analysis, since this would necessarily deprive it of the elements of shock and surprise. But we should ask first why these might be important and effective in the first place.

In his first formulations of analytic technique, Freud saw the aim of interpretation as accessing an unconscious train of thought. Certain words would emerge in the analysand's speech which he termed "switch words": these would function as junction points between disparate chains of representations. The classic examples are in the Dora case. By focusing on a switch word, it would become possible to move from one train of thought to another, unconscious one. The word "fire", for example, in Dora's first dream, would lead to the chain of ideas about "love" and to those about its contrary, "water", both of which articulated sexual themes (Freud, 1905e, p. 72). The effect of this would be surprise, indignation, laughter or other phenomena of subjective division, signalling the discovery of an unconscious truth.

By the mid-1930s, Freud's thinking on interpretation had changed considerably. In his 1937 paper on "Constructions in analysis", for example, he argued that an interpretation did not even have to be true. What mattered would be its effects, and he could quote the famous line from *Hamlet* that the "bait of falsehood had taken a carp of truth" (Freud, 1937d, p. 262). What mattered in an interpretation would not be its material correctness, but rather the effects it produced. This radical idea would have significant consequences for analytic practice: what forms, after all, could such falsehood take? And if what mattered was the effect of interpretation, what limits would there be to its content?

Freud's notoriously inexact interpretation to the Rat Man is a good example of this (Freud, 1909d). Freud emphasised to his analysand that the terms of his marriage had been set by his father, whose pressure to choose one woman rather than another was felt by him as an unbearable dilemma. This remark brought out crucial material linked to the prehistory of the Rat Man: his father's own marital choice and the debts the latter had contracted were clearly a terrible weight on him, which his neurosis attempted to resolve. Yet despite the efficacy of the interpretation it was factually incorrect: the suggestion as to the choice of the analysand's bride came not from the father but the mother.

It was Lacan who brought out this tension between subjective truth and the facts, elaborating the distinctions that Freud had made in the 1937 paper. Commenting on the Rat Man case, he not only observed the accuracy of this "inaccurate" interpretation, but used it as a paradigm to formulate the aims of interpretation: less to reinforce the stagnation of the transference than to always bring the subject back to his history (see "The direction of the treatment and the principles of its power", in: Lacan, 1966, pp. 489–542). Analysis here involves an introduction to the dimension of the Other, the myths, stories, and narratives that predate the subject's birth. These are necessarily beyond the dual relation of analysand-analyst, yet they determine the structure of the symptoms. For Lacan, even when projection is at its height, the subject should be brought back to the positioning of these signifiers.

Despite the importance of the "Constructions" article, within a decade its lessons had all but been forgotten by the analytic mainstream. Analysts who had worked with Freud and who belonged to the first and second generation observed with astonishment how things had changed. The Zürich Congress in 1949 is a benchmark here, as it brought together the old and the new. Michael Balint described how recent analytic practice bore little relation to the technique he knew, which focused on the symptom. Now, he said, analysis involved systematic interpretation of the transference, something that had been previously a sporadic and infrequent action (Balint, 1949, pp. 221–235).

Transference was now seen as the clue to early object relations. Analysts would not simply take their bearings from transference, but would, on the basis of this, communicate hypotheses about the analysand's past to them from this in ways that verged on automatism. Whatever the analysand said or did, it was assumed to be in relation to the analyst, and this had to be vocalised and transmitted for analysis to progress. The contrast here was not a neglect of transference, but rather a neglect of the symptom. And indeed, today, outside the Lacanian orientation, it is rare to find any serious theorisation of what the symptom is or a fidelity to what Lacan called its "formal envelope" ("On my antecedents", in: Lacan, 1966, p. 52).

The debates that followed the Zürich Congress introduced a number of new terms—parameters, interventions, rectifications—designed to make sense of what analysts did that wouldn't count as classical interpretation. Curiously, the more this was explored, the more it became apparent that there had never been such a thing as classical interpretation: Freud and his colleagues worked in different, disparate ways. So now, for many analysts, the solution was simple: rewriting history, classical interpretation just meant the interpretation of transference.

The material of this form of interpretation was also quite particular: less the words of the analysand than the knowledge which was supposedly culled from those words. The emphasis here was less on "sticking to the words" than finding ways to make the analyst's knowledge received properly by the analysand. At the risk of caricaturing, it was almost like the medical conundrum of patient compliance: not which drug to give the patient but how to ensure that they took it. Hence several discussions of interpretation at this time proposed that analytic interventions should be given in "doses", small increments of knowledge that the analysand would be able to digest. Following the model of a TV drama, it was even suggested that interpretations be given in "instalments".

Today, this view is still dominant in many Anglophone contexts of non-Lacanian analysis. At the same time, another perspective has gained ground in some parts of the analytic world, supposedly designed for work with patients suffering from "personality disorders". The idea now is that interpreting will not provide sudden access to some unconscious truth, but rather will form a containing environment for the patient, the kind that was lacking in their infancy. By continuous feedback, the analyst is able to show the patient that they can be understood and that disturbing thoughts and feelings can be processed. This perspective, which stems from Bion's work, is interesting in that it puts the emphasis perhaps more on form than on content. Sadly, the theory behind it assumes that it works because the therapist is more mature and the patient will internalise their more sophisticated way of processing.

Lacan's view of form is quite different. In the 1953 "Rome discourse" (Lacan, 1966, pp. 237–268), he takes up the linguist's differentiation between redundancy and information. Speech may be the vehicle of information, but will also contain noise, additional or unwanted extras that always accompany it. It was exactly this redundant side of speech that interested Lacan, and he saw interpretation as using this as the clue to send the speaker's message back to them "in inverted form". Just as punctuation affects the distribution of meaning in a sentence, analytic scansion aims to reshuffle the sense of the analysand's speech, so their true message can be "delivered".

Interpretation aims here to deprive the speaker of the moorings of their speech, allowing it to become strange and unfamiliar to them. This might involve the repetition of a phrase with a new emphasis or the ending of the session so that what was said could resonate in a new way. Rather than a practice of explaining to the analysand—which would give the analyst the place of master—variable length sessions put the ball in the analysand's court: the analysand and not the analyst is in the position of the producer, having to work with the cut introduced into their discourse.

To take one example, the sentence "I said I'm going to Edinburgh to my mother" has a rather interesting ambiguity. The analysand had intended to report that he had told his mother about his imminent departure to that city, but his words said a bit more than that. He could have said "I told my mother that …" or "I said to my mother that …", but instead the "to my mother" appears at the end of the sentence. This new meaning—that the destination of his journey was his mother—was indexed by the grammatical form. By ending the session at that moment, rather than receiving a nice piece of Oedipal information from the analyst, the analysand has to figure out for himself what the real motive was for his departure.

As Lacan developed his ideas of unconscious desire and language, he emphasised less their congruence than their "incompatibility". Something cannot be said, yet which is nonetheless indexed by speech. Already this idea is present in the "Rome discourse", and it must have surprised some of its readers when, after the sustained emphasis on structural linguistics, Lacan invokes an example of allusiveness from Hindu aesthetics to situate interpretation. This theoretical hypothesis has the strongest consequences for the practice of interpretation: effectively, it rules out interpretations in the form of "Your desire is …" or "You want …". If desire and speech are incompatible, desire can never be reduced to the form of a meaningful proposition. With the above example, to say "You are going to Edinburgh to satisfy your mother" would leave unconscious desire untouched.

Analytic interpretation for Lacan thus took on a new aim: to affect a sense that could not be expressed lexically. We could think here of the cartoon in which two analysts pass each other on the street with a "Good morning". As they walk off, each thinks "What did he mean by that?". Unconscious desire is situated beyond speech, yet since speech is the very medium of analytic work, how can it be used to access that which cannot be said? To respond to this question requires a theory of language, and it is here that we find the key separation between Lacanian work and that of other orientations.

To illustrate and develop these ideas, we can read a clinical case from the literature that Moustapha Safouan has provided an elegant commentary on in his *Études sur l'Oedipe* (1974, pp. 183–205). Californian analyst Norman Reider published "Metaphor as interpretation" in the *International Journal* in 1972. The patient had gone into analysis after her anxiety about the extension of her house had grown out of all proportion since the birth of her third child, her first boy. After listening to the litany of complaints about her architects, her contractors, and her unsympathetic husband, the analyst interpreted quite directly to her that her worries about the house were in fact a displacement of her concerns about damage to her body. The analysand was immediately relieved, admitted that she had always felt there was something wrong with her body, but, too embarrassed to talk any further, broke off the treatment.

After a period of calm, her anger flared up and she returned to the analysis. More material about the body followed: she felt she had damaged herself through masturbation and experienced total anaesthesia during coitus. Afterwards she would masturbate once her husband was asleep, and Reider noted a tension between her "frigidity" and "private" potency. Interpretations of the rather sexualised transference and of her childhood seductiveness and exhibitionism produced little effect.

After a life-threatening event brought about an improvement in her symptoms, she felt ready to leave the analysis yet again, but a new panic kept her there. She now feared that her genitals were irreparably damaged. She perceived a widened introitus in her genitals rather than the "smooth nothingness of a female statue". The effort to avoid thinking about sexuality echoed the mother's imperative "We don't do things like that". She would blank out the sexual characteristics on sculpture, and could even sit next to a one-legged student for a whole term in college without noticing the absence of a limb.

She refused to accept that her mother was a sexual being. If she had slept with the father, there was certainly no question of orgasm, as her mother was far too much of a lady for that. A vaginal orgasm for a woman meant that "something was wrong". The analyst interpreted that she feared the penis, and this would explain her behaviour and denial of sexuality. Her mockery and teasing of the analyst, in turn, was interpreted—tacitly—as follows: she saw her father's penis with awe, then defended herself against her voyeuristic impulse by an aversion and denunciation of the analyst. So, transferentially, she played "a game of peek-a-boo" with him.

The advances that Reider observed in the treatment tended to be swiftly followed by "re-repressions", as if each step forward was followed by a step back. He understood this as the result of her inability to tolerate intense erotic feelings towards another person. This, he would interpret to her, was equivalent to her sense of being damaged. Now, the breakthrough in the analysis occurred one day when Reider broke with his usual style of interpretation. Rather than focusing on the ideas of damage and defence, he simply said, "You know, there is a Japanese saying to the effect that a blind man is not afraid of snakes". This was really the turning point in the treatment.

The analysand now recalled a dream from her adolescence: she was masturbating and a lizard came out of her vagina as she orgasmed and scampered away. She woke in a panic. Reider now realised that he'd been barking up the wrong tree: it wasn't that she wanted a penis, but that she already had one inside, which could be lost if she became excited. Memories and associations followed that linked the idea of masturbation with that of visibility. She remembered a further dream that dated much earlier, to her fourth or fifth year. It took place after her father had bought her a chameleon at a fair which she became very attached to. She kept a thread round its neck so it always remained close to her. During an illness around this time, she had the nightmare that she could not find the chameleon and that it had crawled inside her.

The sexual threads of her symptoms now began to unravel, together with the emergence of new and important material about her father, mother, and sister. But why had the interpretation had such powerful effects? The analyst, after all, had not told her that she believed she had something inside. He had not put forward a construction about her childhood or said anything about her relations with those closest to her. All he had done was quote a two-bit proverb. And yet it was this that changed everything.

The interpretation had not been planned, and was, in Reider's words, "an accidental venture". He was clearly perplexed by its success, and at the end of his paper he tries to make sense of its strange efficacy. Could it have worked because it was impersonal, because it respected the analysand's intelligence and "cultural self-esteem"? These formulations seem a little unconvincing. Was it, he then wonders, because of its "countertransference implications": his mood at the time he heard the proverb himself. Reider practised in Beverly Hills, and, given that the analysis no doubt took place in the late 60s, we could imagine him being at a party of dope-smoking hippies, impressed by the pearls of Eastern wisdom they exchanged with each other.

His embarrassment in explaining the effect of the proverb is patent here. And the subsequent formulations add very little: the metaphor of the blind man and the snakes was based on unconscious phantasy, metaphors have their roots in concern about the body image, and so on. Yet the key feature, as Reider acknowledges, was surely the fact that the interpretation was a metaphor, and the form of metaphor, as he notices, is none other than that of the primary process itself. Rather than naming directly, the interpretation alluded and opened up a space for meaning to emerge.

In contrast to the previous style of interpreting, the proverb was an allusion not an explanation. In a well-known formula, Lacan equated desire and interpretation, in this exact sense: the allusive, enigmatic interpretation mimicked the unconscious process of displacement itself. It showed how the signifier creates the signified, engaging the analysand with the question of how meaning is created. As Safouan observes, it was less the terms that mattered here than the linguistic mechanism of substitution itself. It was this that allowed something else to be heard beyond the analyst's usual explanatory interventions: a new meaning, that of desire. It was in the very linguistic mechanism of the interpretation that unconscious desire could recognise itself.

Interpretation here does not aim to be understood, but to isolate one signifier from another, to separate. It alluded to a point of no knowledge. This separating power of interpretation was what preoccupied Lacan in the 1960s and early 70s. If speech tends to mask the disparity between signifier and signified, how could interpretation untangle them? The answer, for Lacan, lay not in speech but in writing. In speech, there is displacement and movement, non-identity, and difference. But writing, taking as its paradigm the proper name, stays the same: it remains constant from one language to another. This constancy was that of the libido, which would congeal certain signifiers and isolate them from the rest of the signifying chain.

Lacan's idea was that one could try to access the dimension of writing within speech and then, perhaps, bring it back to speech. If writing involved an identity, speech consisted of difference, the famous diacritical characteristics of language that the structuralists had made so much of. Hence his new definition of interpretation: that which lay in between a citation and an enigma. To take an elementary example, the sentence "Cicero has five letters" will be true or false depending on how we situate its reference: if we put citation marks around the word "Cicero", then the sentence is false. But if we don't, and if he indeed has five letters to post, it would come out true. Citation introduces the writing present within speech, a sameness embodied by the identity of the proper name. Enigma, on the other hand, indexes the desire of the Other. For Lacan, this edge between enigma and citation can be elaborated in at least three ways: homophony, grammar, and logic.

Rather than elaborating these three axes further here, let's take a few examples from Lacan's practice. They are taken from Jean Allouch's compendium *Allo Lacan? Certainement Pas* (1998), and give an idea of a style of interpreting which does not aim at education, instruction, or telling the analysand what they are thinking. In fact, the examples bring out the importance of surprise, shock, and displacement, as well as an attention to the absolute particularity of each case.

- In our first example, an analysand complains incessantly about her weight and the fact that her diets keep failing. One day, Lacan says to her "Ask Gloria [his secretary], she knows a diet for slimming [un regime pour maigrir]". The analysand meets Gloria on the way out but hesitates: without asking her anything she leaves and suddenly hears the apostrophe in her analyst's remark: "un regime pour m'aigrir", a diet for becoming embittered.
- For several months an analysand spoke to Lacan about his love for a certain woman. All the material was about her, including an "analysis" of his love, why he had fallen for her, etc. One day he shows up for his session and says "I'm getting married next week". Lacan replies "To whom?".
- An analysand, although immersed in the psychoanalytic world, decides that he has to obtain a diploma in medicine. He registers for medical studies and tells his analyst about his decision. Lacan, in reply, doubles his fee, thus making it materially impossible for the analysand to pursue his studies.
- An analysand enters his session smoking one of the trademark cigars of his analyst. Lacan takes it away from his analysand, stubbing it out in an ashtray with the words "Give that to me … you'll be more comfortable."
- After the death of her analyst, a woman makes a first appointment with Lacan to discuss starting analysis with him. When Lacan understands that the funeral was taking place at that very moment, he asks her if she intended to go. After a moment of uncertainty, she says yes. Lacan asks her if she has a car, and there and then, leaving a packed waiting room, accompanies her to the funeral.
- A very rich man consults Lacan, hoping to start an analysis. When the moment comes to fix the fee, and since it was clear that this man had too much money ever to be able to really pay for anything, Lacan asks him for one symbolic franc per session.

These examples, and the elaborations we have discussed, should make us question the stereotyped image of the Lacanian analyst making wordplays, as if verbal ambiguity was enough to conduct an analysis. Of course, such moments can have all their value, as we saw in the example of the Japanese proverb, but we should remember there that it was precisely this intervention that broke the continuity of the analyst's interpretative style. This very discontinuity introduces something beyond allusion, a theatricality that is certainly present in the examples from Lacan's practice we have given above.

Theatre, after all, may be poetry, but it is never just poetry. It involves the presence of the body in speech, perhaps a mimicry, an exaggeration of tone or gesture, a clowning: like the play-within-the–play of Elizabethan drama or simply the classical form of Hellenistic tragedy and comedy, theatre is a means of conveying truth without saying what truth is. And isn't this why Lacan felt it necessary to introduce a new concept to the debate around interpretation? His notion of the analytic act is about precisely that: the fact that there is something beyond the deciphering of the linguistic mechanisms of the unconscious. Although deciphering the unconscious is part and parcel of every psychoanalysis, the key moments of change involve both more and less than this.

These moments, if they are authentic, are either very brave or very stupid. They aim less to instruct than to change, less to educate or unravel than to separate and shift, less to decipher the unconscious than to respond to it.

References

Allouch, J. (1998). *Allo Lacan? Certainement Pas*. Paris: Epel.

Balint, M. (1949). Changing therapeutical aims and techniques in psychoanalysis. In: M. Balint. *Primary Love and Psycho-Analytic Technique*: 221–235. London: Hogarth, 1952.

Freud, S. (1905e). *Fragment of an analysis of a case of hysteria. S. E., 7*: 1–122. London: Hogarth, 1953.

Freud, S. (1909d). *Notes upon a case of obsessional neurosis. S. E., 10*: 151–318. London: Hogarth, 1955.

Freud, S. (1937d). *Constructions in analysis. S. E., 23*: 1964, 255–269. London: Hogarth.

Lacan, J. (1966). *Écrits*. B. Fink (Trans.). New York: Norton, 2002.

Leader, D. (1996). Strategy, tactics and standard treatment. *Journal of the Centre for Freudian Analysis and Research, 7*: 20–26.

Reider, N. (1972). Metaphor as interpretation. *International Journal of Psychoanalysis, 53*: 463–469.

Safouan, M. (1974). *Études sur l'Oedipe*. Paris: Seuil.

INDEX

Abraham, K. 42, 84
Allouch, J. 91, 93
anxiety 9–11, 16, 62–63, 65, 67, 76–77, 81–82, 88

Balint, M. 86, 93
Bernheim, H. 4–5
Bouvet, M. 42, 54
Breuer, J. 4–5, 21, 55–56, 68

castration 25, 32, 36, 39, 42–45, 54, 59, 66, 73
Charcot, J. M. 3–5, 55
countertransference 73, 81, 90
    see also transference

Darriba, V. 40, 54
death drive 24, 41, 45, 72
    see also drive
desire 41, 44–49, 51–52, 59–67, 71, 77–78, 80, 84, 88, 91

Ding (Thing) 45–51
drive xii, 6, 8–9, 12, 24, 28, 33, 40–45, 48, 50, 52–54, 72
    see also death drive

ego xii, 1, 7–9, 11, 13–16, 19, 21, 24–28, 30, 32, 34, 36, 46, 77, 79, 84
    psychology/psychologist(s) 16–19, 26, 36
    see also super-ego

Fink, B. 21, 37, 54, 63–64, 67–68, 82, 93
Freud, S. xi, 1–21, 23–36, 39–59, 62, 65, 67–74, 79–82, 84–86, 93

Hartmann, H. 27, 36
Hegel, G. W. F. 30, 33
Heimann, P. 81–82

hysteria 3–5, 12, 21, 52, 55–59, 61, 63, 66–68, 93

imaginary xii, 7, 23, 31–32, 34–35, 40, 50
interpretation 15, 36, 64–65, 70–71, 80, 83–91, 93
The Interpretation of Dreams 6, 19, 21, 23, 36

Janet, P. 4
jouissance 48, 51–52, 62–63, 65, 78, 81
Julien, P. 28, 36
Jung, C. G. 6–8, 17, 20–21

Kaplan, R. 39, 54
Klein, M. 19, 25, 42
Kris, E. 18, 26

Lacan, J. xi–xii, 1, 7, 13–14, 17–21, 23–37, 39–52, 54, 58–61, 64–68, 70, 74–76, 78–82, 84–88, 91–93
lack 32, 39, 41–52, 58–59, 61–66, 77
language 15, 17–18, 20, 31, 47–48, 50, 56, 74, 76, 81, 88, 91
Leader, D. xiii, 84, 93
libido 6, 42, 91
    organisation of 42
Loewenstein, R. 26

master signifier 18, 33, 45
    see also signifier
mirror phase 23, 27, 29–31, 34–35

neurosis xi, 27, 55, 57–59, 67–68, 72, 84–85, 93

object 9, 15, 18, 28, 30, 32–33, 35, 39–49, 51–52, 59–67, 78–79
    -cathexis 14–15
    choice 42

(little) a 39–41, 45, 48–49, 51–52, 60–61
    relation(s) 42–43, 45, 47, 86
    relations schools/theories 19, 25, 43–44, 47
obsession(al) 52, 55, 57–59, 61–68, 93
Other xii, 25, 27, 29–30, 33, 59–67, 77–78, 80–81, 85, 91

phantasy xii, 11, 31–32, 35, 60–63, 65–66, 72–73, 78, 90
phobia 10, 12, 18, 57, 67

Rapaport, D. 26, 36
Razavet, J.-C. 42, 54
real xii, 23, 31–32, 41, 44, 47–51, 53, 59, 63, 78, 81
reality 14, 24, 28, 32, 34, 44, 46, 80
Reider, N. 88–90, 93
repetition 33, 41, 49–50, 72
repression 2, 6, 13–15, 19, 56, 58–59, 68, 71, 83, 89
Rome discourse 18, 20, 87–88
Rosenfeld, H. 84

Sachs, H. 84
Safouan, M. 88, 91, 93
Shakespeare, W. 39, 54
signifier 32–34, 40–41, 43, 45, 47–52, 76, 79, 85, 91
    see also master signifier
Soler, C. 64–68
speech 17–18, 20, 52, 74–76, 81, 84, 87–88, 91, 93
subject xii, 9, 19–20, 30, 33, 35, 39, 41–45, 47–48, 50–51, 53–54, 59–61, 63–67, 77, 79–80, 85
sublimation 48–49, 54
superego 15–16, 24–25
    see also ego
symbolic xii, 23, 31–32, 34, 40–41, 43, 47–48, 50, 59

symptom 1–5, 7, 9–10, 12, 16, 27, 55–59, 64, 66, 69, 71–72, 76, 79, 81, 85–86, 89–90

Thing *see Ding*
thing-presentations 14–15
transference 4, 20, 33, 52, 65–66, 69–73, 75–81
    love 33, 77–78, 80, 82
    see also countertransference

unconscious 1–2, 4–21, 23–24, 31–33, 35–36, 43, 47, 50–51, 54, 56, 65–66, 69–70, 80, 83, 93
    desire 88, 91
    phantasy xii, 32, 35, 72–73, 90
    truth 85, 87

Wallon, H. 27–28, 37
Wine, N. 52, 54
word-presentations 14–15, 17